# THE IMMORTAL GAMBLE

"It was a gamble, but a perfectly legitimate gamble."
          MR. WINSTON CHURCHILL *in the House of Commons.*

STORES BURNING AT SUVLA. FORE-TURRET OF H.M.S. "CORNWALLIS," THE LAST SHIP TO LEAVE SUVLA BAY.

*Central News, Ltd.*

# THE IMMORTAL GAMBLE

AND THE PART PLAYED IN IT BY
H.M.S. "CORNWALLIS"

BY

A. T. STEWART
ACTING COMMANDER, R.N.

AND

THE REV. C. J. E. PESHALL, B.A.
CHAPLAIN, R.N.

The Naval & Military Press Ltd

Published by
**The Naval & Military Press Ltd**
Unit 10 Ridgewood Industrial Park,
Uckfield, East Sussex,
TN22 5QE England
Tel: +44 (0) 1825 749494
Fax: +44 (0) 1825 765701
www.naval-military-press.com
www.military-genealogy.com
www.militarymaproom.com

*In reprinting in facsimile from the original, any imperfections are inevitably reproduced and the quality may fall short of modern type and cartographic standards.*

## Dedication

TO THE IMPERISHABLE MEMORY OF OUR
COMRADES OF BOTH SERVICES AND ALL
ARMS OF OUR EMPIRE AND OF FRANCE,
WHO FELL ON THE FIELD OF HONOUR
AT GALLIPOLI

## PREFACE

H.M.S. *CORNWALLIS* played her part in the immortal gamble for a longer space of time than any other battleship. From her fore-turret was fired the first shot of the first day's long-range bombardment of the outer forts. She arrived but two days later than the *Vengeance*, the first battleship on the scene of action in the Ægean, and was the last to leave Suvla Bay after the evacuation, or, as the authorities prefer to call it, withdrawal. What's in a name ? We heard a charming Canadian nurse at Mudros describe the historical operation as a " real slick vamooze." It is not a bad definition. Evacuation, withdrawal, or vamooze, the *Cornwallis* was in the midst of it, and it is with the conviction that there are very many people who will be interested in this record of her service during a long and strenuous twelve months that the writers have massed their experiences.

Just as every goose is a swan to the parent

birds, so the average Captain is the one and only Captain in the fleet to the average ship's company. The apt characterization of one of our marines will delineate Captain Davidson for you as no modern photograph could do.

Our marine was engaged in a belauding competition with an old-time shipmate from the *Albion*, a horny pensioner who since his retirement had conducted a hair-dressing business in a remote Devonshire village, and therefore might be said to know something of masculine nature.

"Now our skipper is what you might call a 'umanitar-i-an. A 'umanitar-i-an is wot 'ee is."

The marine from the *Albion* looked what he was—puzzled. He had heard some long words in his day—you can't keep a hair-dressing shop in Devon without coming across patrons who use words of three syllables. Martinets he knew all about, dis-cip-plinarians too, but *this*, this was something altogether new. Proper New Navy, no doubt—came in with oil-driven ships and electric capstans.

"Your skipper, is 'ee a 'umanitar-i-an?" pursued the *Cornwallis* relentlessly.

The marine from the *Albion* took some time to

reply. He had been long enough in the world to realize that there is an ignorance that precedes knowledge just as there is an ignorance that comes after it.

"'Ee might be and 'ee might not," he said at last darkly.

To speak of the way in which Captain Davidson handled his ship during the many days we were under fire would be to grow technical, and technicalities the armchair strategist—for whom this book is primarily written—bars. From the onset of the operations, Captain Davidson saw that the vital principle on which to work was that of constant movement. We were constantly kept moving. If we were at rest when the Turks began shelling, we at once put on speed, and our failure to be hit more than three times is due to the consistent following out of this rule.

The V.C., the D.S.O., the D.S.C., the D.S.M., and Mentions in Despatches, were all won by officers and men of the *Cornwallis*; and when it is remembered that naval honours are not dealt out with the lavish prodigality of army awards, it will be recognized that the old ship has seen some fighting.

Not very long ago a helpful publisher (not ours) advised us on the best way to tackle these experiences, a way by which we should insure what he called " a large reading public." Strong, terse English he advocated as being of first importance; the personal view must be put with freshness and originality; the war itself or the education of people who would win battles, even the spirit that is necessary and is called patriotism, was nothing provided sufficient sensation were forthcoming—" sensation," he added, " stimulated by words."

It seemed to us non-literary people like reducing everything to the level of the cinema. All that matters: the strategy, the tactics, the organization, the conduct of operations—must we avoid them ?

Have they no interest for the general reader ? Does he really demand little tags of camp jokes and funny incidents—a sort of Charlie Chaplin war ? Our publisher, guide, and philosopher bade us abjure the weary routine, the deadly horrors, the ghastly details. There must be no suffering, no blood, nothing to shock.

But war is a dreadful business, and only war correspondents can make a spectacle of it.

## PREFACE

In putting together this record, we have not been entirely successful in bringing to light the doings of those members of the ship who served under conditions and in scenes in which the writers were not present. The ship herself represented a base, and some of her company were frequently detached on services out of sight, but they were always in touch with, and dependent on, their base for their organization and supply. We had men in the beach parties at Gallipoli practically throughout the occupation—seamen, boats' crews, signalmen, and occasionally officers. Everyone was ready for extra service, and volunteers were always forthcoming. For the mine-sweeping which went on under our eyes men were detached, as they were to trawlers, tugs, lighters, and other small craft, and these representatives, whose work is to the credit of us all, shared in many wonderful events at which the *Cornwallis* herself was not present.

Our navigator, Lieutenant-Commander J. W. Clayton, R.N., assisted by Midshipman Voelcker, R.N., drew our excellent map, than which we have seen none better. To them, as to all those who contributed to the making of this record by accounts of their experiences and by photographs, the authors express their thanks and indebtedness; and if the splicing together of the many yarns reminds you all of the old seafaring adage, "Every man a rope and the cook to the fore-sheet," it will not matter if the result is interesting.

And now, without any further preliminaries, we will dig our toes in and haul away on the fall.

A. T. S.
C. J. E. P.

# CONTENTS

| CHAPTER | PAGE |
|---|---|
| I. THE CAST IS THROWN | 1 |
| II. THE PRELIMINARY LANDINGS | 19 |
| III. THE BATTLE OF THE NARROWS | 45 |
| IV. STEPPING-STONES | 59 |
| V. THE GREAT LANDING | 71 |
| VI. SIDELIGHTS | 97 |
| VII. OF THE DEAD—AND OF THE LIVING | 125 |
| VIII. THE DIN OF ARMS | 143 |
| IX. THE LOSS OF THE "GOLIATH" | 167 |
| X. THE COMING OF THE GERMAN SUBMARINES | 179 |
| XI. IN HARBOUR | 196 |
| XII. OF DOING NOTHING | 214 |
| XIII. THE EVACUATION OF SUVLA AND ANZAC | 223 |
| XIV. ASHORE AT SUVLA | 246 |
| XV. THE HAND IS PLAYED | 256 |
| "DIES IRÆ" | 262 |
| LIST OF HONOURS, H.M.S. "CORNWALLIS," DURING 1915 | 264 |
| OFFICERS WHO SERVED IN H.M.S. "CORNWALLIS" BETWEEN DECEMBER, 1914, AND MARCH, 1916 | 268 |

# LIST OF ILLUSTRATIONS

| | |
|---|---|
| STORES BURNING AT SUVLA | *Frontispiece* |
| | PAGE |
| AFTER COALING SHIP AT SKYROS | 8 |
| QUARTER-DECK OF H.M.S. "CORNWALLIS" DURING AMMUNITIONING | 9 |
| OFFICER'S CABIN WRECKED BY A SHELL | 32 |
| FORT 6, KUM KALE | |
| THE DESTRUCTION OF KUM KALE | *Between 32 and 33* |
| MINE-SWEEPING TRAWLERS | |
| PREPARING TO LAND 2ND BATTALION SOUTH WALES BORDERERS ON APRIL 25TH, 1915 | 33 |
| STONE TAKEN FROM FORT 1 AND SET UP ON QUARTER-DECK OF H.M.S. "CORNWALLIS" | 80 |
| BOATS FROM "CORNWALLIS" LANDING MARINE BRIGADE | 81 |
| ROYAL MARINES ON BOARD H.M.S. "CORNWALLIS" | 81 |
| A BRITISH BATTLE-CRUISER IN THE DARDANELLES FIRING AT THE NARROWS FORT | 88 |
| RUINS OF THE FORTRESS OF SEDD-UL-BAHR | 89 |
| STORES ON V BEACH AND THE "RIVER CLYDE" | 128 |
| EXTERIOR OF SEDD-UL-BAHR FORT | 129 |
| INTERIOR OF SEDD-UL-BAHR FORT | 129 |
| GUN KNOCKED OUT BY H.M.S. "CORNWALLIS" | 136 |

# LIST OF ILLUSTRATIONS

|  | PAGE |
|---|---|
| FO'C'SLE OF "CORNWALLIS" DURING A LULL IN THE BOMBARDMENT | 137 |
| TURKISH GUN IN RUINS OF SEDD-UL-BAHR FORT | 144 |
| SEDD-UL-BAHR IN THE DISTANCE | 145 |
| ON BOARD HOSPITAL SHIP "DEVANHA" | 152 |
| WOUNDED FROM THE SUVLA LANDING | 153 |
| WOUNDED COMING IN-BOARD | 153 |
| CORN-THRESHING WITH OXEN AND SLEDGE | 176 |
| SUNSET IN MUDROS HARBOUR | 177 |
| X BEACH | 184 |
| A FRENCH GUN AT GALLIPOLI | 185 |
| HIC JACET H.M.S. "MAJESTIC" | 200 |
| A "REST" CAMP | 201 |
| LOADING PATIENTS INTO HOSPITAL SHIP | 208 |
| THE ROUGH HILLS OF GALLIPOLI | 209 |
| GENERAL BIRDWOOD ON BOARD THE "CORNWALLIS" | 224 |
| LORD KITCHENER AT GALLIPOLI | 225 |
| A PARTING SHOT FROM THE TURKS | 232 |
| H.M.S. "CORNWALLIS" FIRING AT THE TURKS IN THE MOUNTAINS | 233 |
| THE ARMS OF THE CORNWALLIS FAMILY<br>Taken from the tompion of a 12-inch gun on board H.M.S. "Cornwallis" | *On title-page and on the cover* |

*Sketch-map on page xvi.*

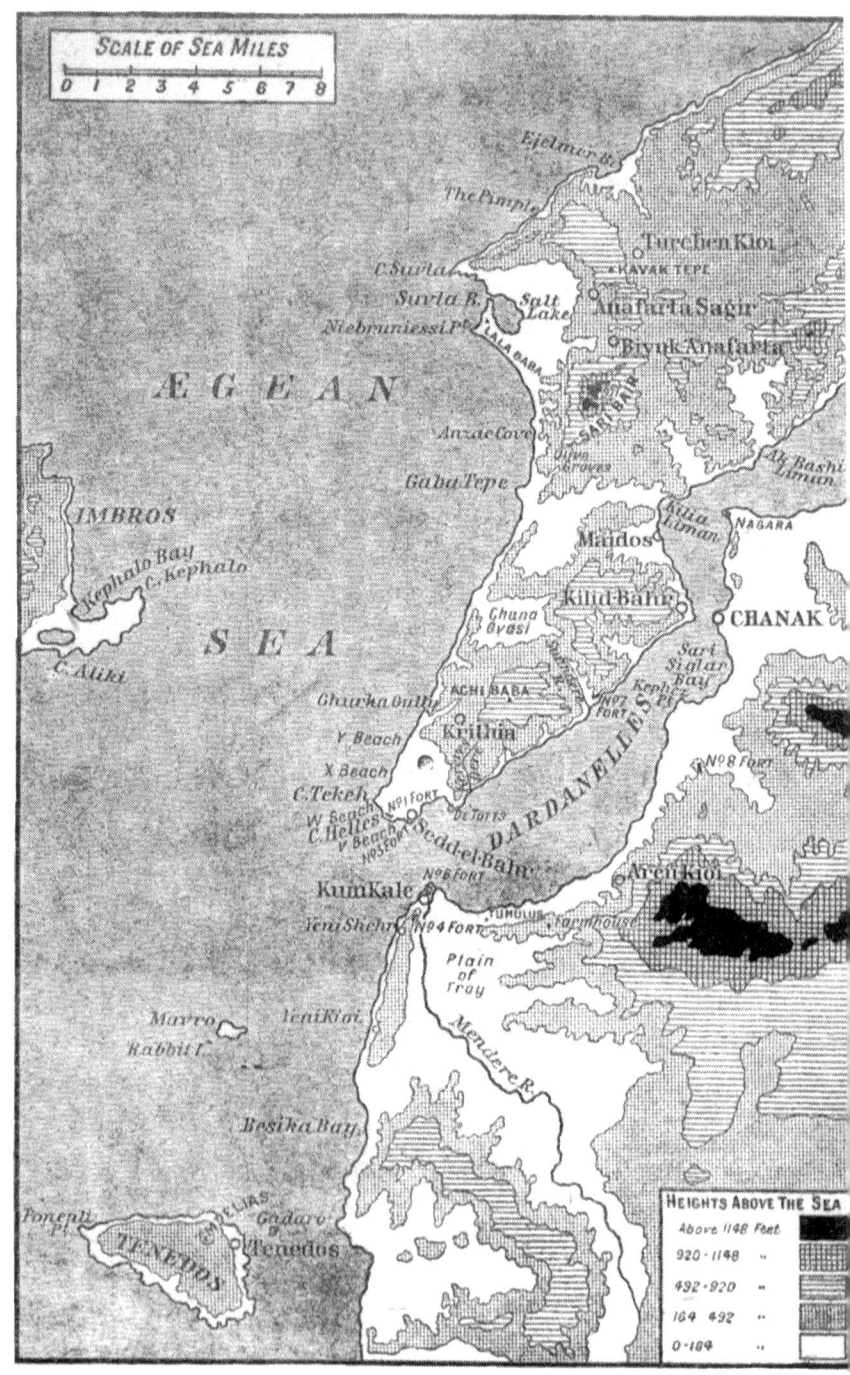

SKETCH-MAP OF THE DARDANELLES AND VICINITY.

# THE IMMORTAL GAMBLE

## CHAPTER I

### THE CAST IS THROWN

THE early days of our commission (December, 1914) as an old type of ship unwanted in the Grand Fleet appeared to doom us to the strip of water blessed for its narrowness by Tennyson, who, all the same, had sufficient breadth of space about him to wish, as we did, " they were a whole Atlantic broad." What with mines in the heat of " unfortunate disasters " and German submarines in flux, the Channel was no place for a middle-aged battleship.

Christmas, 1914, we spent " somewhere in Ireland," and on reaching the lonely spot selected as our temporary base—we were calibrating and shaking down generally after a refit of months—we found our secret corner not quite so secret as we thought.

In the bay a beautiful steam yacht lay at anchor

—an American. Curious time of year for yachting! Curious tastes the owner had in many ways. He liked yachting in war-time, preferred it, in fact. Mines? Wal, the old hooker had escaped up to date, and a mine was no tougher proposition than they had expected!

A rambling explanation of boiler defects gave us an opportunity to offer technical advice and assistance, and a visit to the yacht introduced us to a guest whose name was well known to us all. It was the same as that of a notorious personage recently shot as a rebel for his connection with the Sinn Fein rising. The more we saw of the ship, the owner, and his friend, the less we liked the trio. The unsatisfactorily explained presence was reported, but what further steps were taken, if any, we never heard.

Up and down our prescribed area we wandered, driven by the necessities of gunnery, and for days (as now it seems to us) mail day was never mail day, and the decks and cabins were always awash. On the last day of December one of the guns' crew was swept overboard—our first casualty.

Captain Le Mesurier left us in January, 1915, and was succeeded by Captain A. P. Davidson, in the midst of a busy week of coaling and com-

## THE CAST IS THROWN

pleting with various stores, which, by reason of their quantity, were regarded in the light of coming events by the hopeful and as a natural sequence by the rest. For a pre-Dreadnought like ourselves, what was there but some secondary rôle? It was quite on the cards that we might go through the whole war without firing a shot.

And thus it was when the end of January found us on our way abroad everyone hailed the leaving behind of the dull, cold, winter weather with joy. We were bound for a place where the sun shines, and at the back of everyone's mind was the growing conviction that we, "the surplus," the hitherto unwanted, were going to strike a blow for the country. Just how we were to hit out or where, the Ward-room argued o' nights as only Ward-rooms can.

The Chief said he believed we were going through the Canal and into the Gulf; the Pay. thought we were sure to fetch up in the Adriatic, where we should account for a goodly proportion of the Austrian fleet; the R.N.R. Lieutenant, whom we call "little" because of his six feet three of inches and "heathen" because of his language, said he was certain—and he was certain because he had dreamed it three nights running—

we were going to Constantinople on a non-stop run.

Only the skipper knew, and he didn't tell.

The Gunnery-Lieutenant looked forward to reading the Germo-Turk a lesson with a 12-inch gun, and even the Pessimist—of course we have a Pessimist: what Ward-room has not?—found the prospect pleasing, and went so far as to say it was a great stroke of luck. He had made up his mind long ago that nothing more than a shot at Zeebrugge would ever come our way—most likely not even that.

The first day out we intercepted a signal from the C.-in-C. to the *Lion* and *Indomitable* asking for number of killed and wounded, and from that gathered there had been an engagement somewhere.

No letters reached us of course, no telegrams or signals—a real hardship in stirring times. The silence was broken at last by a communicative collier off Quiberon Bay, who gave us the news of the fight in the North Sea and the sinking of the *Blucher*. We got our first message from Poldhu, twopence coloured, like the *Daily Wail*, only more so. It mentioned a big German attack on the Allies, which was repulsed with a loss to the enemy of 20,000.

## THE CAST IS THROWN

"I hope it's all true," said the Pessimist dubiously.

Whilst the rest of us played bridge he sat meditating for a long time, and then tried (oh, how vainly!) to play "Destiny" on an unevenly balanced piano whose middle register was somewhat thickened by the doubtful lubrication of a spilt whisky-and-soda.

"Don't breathe so hard!" snapped the Fleet-Surgeon. "You put me off scoring."

\* \* \* \* \* \*

Owing to the constant coaling—war is not peace, you know, any more than cleanliness is really next to godliness—the ship remained very dirty. Four coalings in two weeks becomes nightmare-like. And at Gibraltar we coaled again.

The *Carmania* and *Sydney* lay at their moorings, the *Dartmouth* and *Cumberland* were coaling like ourselves, and off the Ragged Staff several captured German steamers were secured. Good-sized, serviceable vessels, it did one good to look at them.

The *Vengeance* left Gibraltar for Malta a little ahead of us, and we were in hopes of overtaking her, so kept up a good fifteen knots all the way. She had too great a start, and as we entered the

Grand Harbour at Valetta, we saw her already coaling. We took up a berth close to the French flagship, the *Paris*.

Our French allies were using Malta as a base for their Eastern operations, and their navy was well represented. Battleships, battle-cruisers, cruisers and their attendant T.B.D.'s, T.B.'s and store-ships, met the eye everywhere. The *Jean Bart* and several T.B.D's. were refitting. The *Cornwallis*, *Vengeance*, and *Indefatigable* appeared to be the only British ships in harbour.

We arrived at Skyros, a lovely little almost landlocked bay, with high hills around covered with juniper scrub, on February 9th, and anchored in company with the French fleet: the *Gaulois* (Flag), *Suffren*, *St. Louis*, and *Charlemagne*, veterans like ourselves, milestones on the path of pre-Dreadnought construction.

We knew by this time what we were all there for—to try and force the Dardanelles, and afterwards settle an account to civilization long overdue. All roads led now to the Mediterranean. Big ships, little ships, all sorts and kinds of craft moved eastward.

One early morning gave us a surprising vision— the *Dublin* turned Futurist. We hardly knew her in a fantastic disguise of æsthetic splashes and smears of paint. When our flagship arrived similarly decorated, the very plates of the staid old *Cornwallis* quivered in protest. Not for her the willing adoption of so bizarre a garb. A sombre even grey suits some styles of beauty, and mutton dressed lamb-fashion is always mutton. We decided to " Wait and see."

In the dusk of a perfect day we shaped our course for Tenedos, steaming quietly through the purple-black water in which the stars reflected themselves and outshone the glittering thread of silver in our wake.

Now and again a far, faint searchlight cut the darkness, like crab's eyes gleaming phosphorescent from the deeps of a rocky pool; a trawler gave greeting as she fussed away to port, and the soft beat of her engines mingled with our own.

"I am coming," they seemed to drone cheerily. "You can't get along without me."

Gradually the combined fleets assembled—an interesting and varied collection of types, mostly pre-Dreadnoughts " of small military value," dating back into the nineties. And after weary weeks of patrolling the submarine-infested Channel back and forth, forth and back, this heaven-sent chance of adding the name of the old "Corned beef" to the pages of a history so gloriously inscribed as that of the Dardanelles seemed the opportunity of a lifetime.

One afternoon a T.B.D. came alongside to take some of our officers and gun-layers to view the nut we hoped to crack. Strict orders were given not to go in close and to avoid drawing the enemy's fire.

It was not possible to do more than pick out general outlines and features. One saw, or thought one saw, an ascent that was steep from every shore and hills that were fairly high. The Asiatic side of the Straits is dominated by the European, and from the contour of the low-lying foreground it was not difficult to place amidst a rampart jumble of rises, ravines, and gullies, spurs leading to backblocks threaded by small rivers and a Never-Never country interspersed by belts of trees. The Pessimist, in unusually hopeful mood, saw more than this. He traced roads winding like an apple-paring thrown over the shoulder. He could see the loops, he said, quite distinctly.

The northern and southern masonry forts, Sedd-ul-Bahr (the name means "barrier of the

AFTER COALING SHIP AT SKYROS.
Shows many members of ship's company who were killed and wounded at Gallipoli.

QUARTER-DECK OF H.M.S. "CORNWALLIS" DURING AMMUNITIONING AT PORT MUDROS.
12-inch projectiles in the foreground.

sea ") and Kum Kale, stood out boldly clear. Grey and primitively square, as if cut from the hillside itself, the details of their rough architecture was sharply defined.

The eternal greatness of the deeds of our sailors and soldiers at Gallipoli have made it impossible for that sepulchre of our hopes to remain the mere geographical expression it used to be. Everyone understands the lie of the land —the narrow peninsula running south-westward into the Ægean Sea, separated from the Asiatic coast by the Dardanelles. Distances, too, are thrummed into our brains—the three to twelve miles wide Peninsula, the forty miles long and from one to four miles wide Straits. Everyone knows it, and therefore it is not necessary to go into careful geographical details.

As we saw it then the entrance to the famous marine pathway lay flooded with sunlight. The high airs from the watershed blew down on it on their way across the Ægean. All was still, still as death, save for the endless movement of many seabirds and the soft distant murmur of the waves.

On such a day the *Argo* sailed to gain the Golden Fleece, following to its end the winding waterway; down the narrow strait journeyed Hercules to wrest the Magic Belt. Almost within sight was the Troy of Agamemnon's besieging. The romance of centuries enwrapped the place. And we were there in all our modernity to take it or die.

What we thought of our chances of forcing a strait believed by every Turk to be impregnable is not for discussion. Visions of the censor's blue pencil deter comprehensive dissection of the knotty subject. Besides—ours was not to make reply.

On the 18th February we received orders for the operations which were to begin the historical attempt, and next day at about 10 a.m. the first shot of the bombardment was fired by the *Cornwallis* and the first hit scored on the fort aimed at—Orkanieh.

The first phase was a long-range bombardment at 10,000 to 12,000 yards, undertaken by ourselves, the *Triumph*, *Inflexible*, *Vengeance* (flying the flag of Vice-Admiral De Robeck), *Suffren*, and later the *Albion* joined in.

The *Triumph*, firing at Number 1 Fort, was having a difficult time of it, for the so-called fort was well hidden and hard to make out. At

## THE CAST IS THROWN

midday she moved farther north, and the *Inflexible* took her place. The latter was also firing at Number 3 Fort, which lay on the shore at the foot of Sedd-ul-Bahr.

After aeroplane reports had been received, a closer attack was made. A French ship advanced supported by the *Vengeance* and *Cornwallis*, and by gradually decreasing ranges our ship reached the minimum range of the day—about 3,700 yards.

Until we closed in there was no movement at all in the forts, and it was an exciting moment when they opened fire on us at a range of 5,000 yards. The majority of the shots were aimed at the *Vengeance*, a few at the *Agamemnon* (which arrived in the afternoon), and six at the *Cornwallis*, but none of them fell within 100 yards of us.

For all on board, with the exception of the Captain, it was the first time under fire, and everybody felt his own particular form of tension and excitement as we watched and waited for the flash of the guns in the forts and the fall of the shell.

The tremendous roaring explosions of many 12-inch guns firing at once came back in droning currents of sound which beat in echoes on the air like waves on a stony beach. Our heavy shell all burst well, throwing up immense clouds of smoke and dust. Earthworks did not suffer so much, but the masonry forts of Sedd-ul-Bahr and Kum Kale soon showed signs of wear and tear. The French shells were not so spectacular as ours, and gave off very little smoke.

We were at "Action Stations" all day, and there was no chance for regular meals. The men were fed where they were—round the guns, in the tops, and at all stations. We could not smoke either, and a pipe to a sailor is a sort of pocket philosopher—a wiser than Socrates really, for it never asks questions.

During the afternoon the recently launched super-Dreadnought, *Queen Elizabeth*, paid a surprise call. Majestic and aloof, she lay far off, as though blessing our endeavours, taking no part in the proceedings herself.

When the newspapers began to come out from home most of us became rather " fed up " with what the *Daily Wail* says we call " Big Lizzie," a name evolved in Fleet Street and not in the fleet; but as we saw her for the first time, I think we all felt a little thrill. It might have been

## THE CAST IS THROWN

pride, it might have been envy, it might have been triumph, but it was a thrill all right.

This was the splendid ship's first commission. For the first time the sea took toll of her, and just as it is when anyone young and strong and valiant goes forth into the world with Fortune creeping behind to cast a capricious transformation over the history, so the *Queen Elizabeth* was commencing her adventurous separate existence.

In the heyday of youth every battleship looks able to withstand the silent challenge of time. We had watched all classes ageing steadily and passing away from the wide waters that were theirs, and yet we all thought how impossible it was that the wonderful *Queen Elizabeth*, as epoch-making a craft as the original Dreadnought, should ever become obsolete. The years must be good to her and pass her lightly. So royal a vessel could never fall the ignominious prey of shipbreakers.

Like her sister ships, the *Queen Elizabeth* is oil-driven, an experiment which, on anything of a scale, has been long in the making with us. How many years is it since the Black Sea traders called the wells of Baku to their aid ?

At night the fleet put to sea. A strong southerly gale sprang up, and our chances of continuing the bombardment next day did not look too bright. The Turks would be boasting they had driven us off! But perhaps at the back of their minds they realized we meant business. They must have had a good few casualties as a beginning.

The fleet gathered off Rabbit Island on February 20th, but returned immediately to the anchorage off the northern shore of Tenedos. In the afternoon the Admiral called a council of Captains, when the plans and orders for the second bombardment were promulgated.

The sea was still too rough for any hope of continuing our cut-short operations. Even in calm weather the odds are in favour of forts when attacked by ships, but when a big sea makes a ship an unsteady platform, it is mere waste of ammunition to attempt a bombardment.

On the Sunday night the fleet put to sea in a heavy gale. The seas were short and big, and a four-ton launch with a ton of water in her was moved on the boat-deck of the *Cornwallis* two feet aft and lifted four feet in the air.

The next day was a *dies non* as far as bombarding was concerned, the next also, and it was not

## THE CAST IS THROWN

until February 25th that the weather improved and operations were able to begin again.

Time was fighting on the side of the Turks. The enforced delay had given them opportunities to make good much of the damage done.

As we took up our positions for long-range bombardment, the forts were ready to deal with us. Fort Number 1 opened by firing on the *Agamemnon* and the *Gaulois*, and for two and a half hours a give-and-take battle ensued.

The *Queen Elizabeth* engaged Fort 3 and then Fort 1, which the *Agamemnon* also tackled, and we watched, from where we lay-to, at about 14,000 yards off, the firing of the *Queen Elizabeth* at 13,000 yards. The 1,950-pound shell bursting was appalling. As each exploded it seemed as if some vast crater had been set in eruption. The accuracy was excellent, and time after time the shells fell on the forts. Without doubt one of the big guns was knocked out in Fort 1.

And with this titanic hammering there was no sound. That struck one as the most curious feature of the whole spectacle. There was no sound. With the wind blowing straight off the land we could not hear anything.

The fort got the range of the *Agamemnon*. She was hit several times, and lost three killed and nine wounded; the *Gaulois*, too, was struck, and her casualties totalled eight killed and many wounded. Not to be out of it, a boy in our ship caught his arm in the cage of the after-turret and was badly lacerated.

At midday the *Vengeance* led the *Cornwallis* for the first close in run at twelve knots, and taking station at half a mile, we opened at 6,000 yards, and fairly poured it in on Forts 4 and 1 in salvoes of 12 and 6-inch. All the time Fort 6 at Kum Kale fired at both ships.

A shot from our fore-turret capsized one gun in Fort 4, and later on we put a beauty on a gun in Number 1. The 6-inch salvoes fell in bunches all round the embrasures, and during the run, which lasted about twenty-five minutes, we fired one hundred and forty rounds of 12 and 6-inch. Two shots passed us very close. One just missed the bow, and the other, close to the foretop, fell over.

We all believe that our fire silenced the two forts, and certain it was that no shot was fired again that day from any of them.

As we came out, the next group of ships had

THE CAST IS THROWN

orders to run close in. The *Suffren*, flying the flag of that fine type of fighting Frenchman, Admiral Guépratte, made beautiful shooting, fast and accurate. The *Triumph* and *Albion* engaged Forts 3 and 6 to complete the destruction, and at dusk the *Inflexible* and *Vengeance* went close in shore and observed no signs of activity. The forts were a mass of ruins. Devastation and desolation reigned supreme.

The mine-sweepers began their dangerous work as we returned to our anchorage, and against the sky the lurid glare of fires burning in Sedd-ul-Bahr and Kum Kale turned the dusk to day, taking the place of the searchlights which, before the 19th, had cast their glare over the water.

When the return of ammunition was made, exception was taken by the flagship to the amount expended by the *Cornwallis*. That was but one of our stumbling-blocks—limited ammunition. The country knows this by now. It is no secret. But in the early days of the immortal gamble the lesson had not been learned that without unstinted ammunition ships are unable to do damage, just as infantry attacks are futile without unlimited artillery preparation. The Turk sticks to his guns, and it is necessary to land a shell on the gun itself. Many shells go close, and on earthworks do little or no harm at all.

Just here we were brought up by the outspoken criticism of the Pessimist, who, uninvited, was overlooking this manuscript.

"It's no use," he said positively, "describing a bombardment to people who most likely don't possess the bombardment feeling. The bombardment feeling cannot be passed on by books."

## CHAPTER II

### THE PRELIMINARY LANDINGS

THE next day, February 27th, four ships went inside the Straits and covered the mine-sweepers, and at noon we were ordered to protect a demolition party from the *Vengeance*, which landed at Kum Kale. A similar expedition set out from the *Irresistible* for Sedd-ul-Bahr.

The distance between Kum Kale and Fort 4, the objective of the men from the *Vengeance*, is about one and a half miles, and between the two lies a typical Mahommedan cemetery, with the usual tall white headstones and their uncanny looking head-like knobs standing sentinel.

Behind the cemetery runs the Mendere River, which was crossed by a bridge, demolished by the French later, leading to the road which was the main artery from Kum Kale to the interior. Rising high above Fort 4, as one followed the coast-line, the village of Yeni Shehir, with its nine picturesque windmills outlined against the sky, clung to the hillside like a bee on the heather-bell.

Outside the village of Kum Kale the small party from the *Vengeance*, advancing in open order, was attacked by the rifle fire of the enemy; but they made their way up to the fort, and from our distant vantage ground we could see some-one—an officer evidently*—go forward at the double across two fields until he reached an outwork which concealed a howitzer. A charge of gun-cotton in the gun, a slow match, and a quick run to the foot of the mound—the deed was done!

Next we saw the whole party go forward one hundred and fifty yards, which brought them to the big left-hand gun in Fort 4, and it went the way of the other. By this time the Turks had opened a hot fire on the destructionists, and the worst of it came from the village on the hill. Immediately the *Dublin* fired at the line of windmills with 6-inch. The signal was scarcely made before she opened fire, and bang, bang, bang—three windmills just slid off the edge of the top of the hill, crumbling as they

* Lieutenant - Commander Robinson, now V.C. and Commander.

## THE PRELIMINARY LANDINGS

went, for all the world as though a giant hand had pushed them over. Six out of nine were brought down in half a minute—a smart bit of work. The *Cornwallis* bagged a windmill too, and the *Dublin* put a few shots into Yeni Shehir.

Meanwhile the gallant little company straggled back to the sea, and a considerable number of Turks had collected with the object of cutting off the landing party. The shell fire of the *Vengeance* and supporting destroyers had something to say to this, and presently the marines gained the boats, with the loss of one sergeant killed and two privates wounded.

The orders for the *Irresistible* landing party were to blow up any gun they might find in Fort 3, Sedd-ul-Bahr; and they evidently got into the magazines, for there were four explosions, and the first was terrific—we had never heard anything like it. There was a sudden crack, as loud and dull as thunder, and an enormous rolling cloud of white smoke that swelled and swelled. Stones and masonry in chunks flew out into the sea for hundreds of yards.

When we could distinguish anything, we realized that practically the whole fort had gone—a ruin marked it. The battery had disappeared.

The "barrier of the sea" was a barrier no more. Was it strange that some of us saw in its fall the casting down of the barrier to our sea power?

The sweeping of the lower portion of the Straits was the next item in the majestic programme, and after that loomed the tackling of the forts at the Narrows, known to be far stronger and more formidable than the sentinels at the entrance.

All that night the *Cornwallis* patrolled the north side of the entrance, and looked forward to another coaling. We coaled incessantly, for keeping bunkers full is a partial protection. In long-range fighting, what is feared is shots falling on the deck and penetrating vital parts, and as an extra precaution sandbags and cables strewed the decks. So far we congratulated ourselves on our luck, and as we did so we touched what little wood we had left in the Ward-room. The ship had been well in the fore-front and had not been hit.

The ammunition bogey, which later assumed grisly proportions, shaped itself. The ill-conditioned bugbear did not take into account the fact that results on forts are undoubtedly less

## THE PRELIMINARY LANDINGS 23

than in ship fighting, when every shot tells more or less. With us it was often less, and a number of good shots merely hit the feet thick earthworks, and the damage was nil.

Saturday, February 28th, saw us patrolling till noon, when we closed the entrance with the object of covering a further demolition party from the *Vengeance*, which was to complete the destruction so well begun in Fort 4; but, unfortunately, the weather was too bad for the landing to take place.

Never was there a region of such quick changes! It blew alternately from north, east, or south, and chopped round from one to the other in a few hours. The sea got up with lightning celerity, and with the wind at north, the temperature in those February days went down to nearly freezing. When a calm ensued out came the sun, and it was a summer's day.

The light was too bad for us to fire on our frequent target, Aren Keui, a village it became a habit with us to bombard. It lay on the Asiatic shore, six miles from Kum Kale, on the slope of the hills where they dipped to the water, and here, in a network of knolls and nullahs contrived by nature for the concealment of field batteries and fixed guns, was a hornet's nest we longed to disperse.

On the European side, under the lee of the old fort, the *Irresistible* landed her second party at Sedd-ul-Bahr, and in spite of strong opposition and continuous sniping, the demolishers contrived to blow up seven howitzers and return to the ship with no casualties at all.

Heavy weather prevented a proposed landing of the Royal Marine Brigade at Forts 1 and 2, and we went off to coal, during the process of which we had the misfortune to lose one of our best petty officers, T. Joughlin. The coaling derrick jambed, and Joughlin swung himself on to the spar of the derrick. He had scarcely overhauled the whip when he seemed to grow tired; he may have had cramp; we could not tell. He let go, and fell fifty feet into the collier alongside, breaking his neck. He was a great worker, and when in charge of the hold during coaling the foretopmen led the others in the amount got on board.

We put to sea in the evening, and Joughlin was buried off Tenedos. The wind had dropped, the sea was dead calm, and a full moon reflected itself in the water. Every man in the

THE PRELIMINARY LANDINGS 25

ship not on watch was present on the quarter-deck.

Not a sound was heard throughout the service, and the shadows drawing about the lonely figure covered with the flag emphasized for us in some strange, unexplainable way the chances of the great gamble in which we were engaged. Joughlin had not lived to see the hand played out. Should we! Should we!

And behind the chaplain's book a little electric torch gleamed like a beacon of hope. It never went out. Brightly it glowed, shining aslant on the deep sweet colours of the proudest robe in which the dead can lie enwrapped.

Silently the body was committed and plunged into the deep. There was a break up of the moonlit surface, and then around the place of the passing the water spread calm again in a profound and noble repose.

All that night we patrolled off the Straits on the south side, and just before midnight heard firing within—field batteries warming up our patrol destroyers and mine-sweepers.

On the 2nd March we were at it again, this time inside the entrance engaging the batteries. We fired 6-inch on the supposed position of some small guns that constantly fired at us, and they stopped off after firing about eight shots. Then we fired more 6-inch at another imagined battery—our imagination these days would have satisfied a Napoleon—and the *Canopus* and *Swiftsure* took on at long range a fort higher up —Number 8, we called it. Number 8 was replying whole-heartedly, and managed to hit the two ships four times each. The *Canopus* had her maintopmast shot away at the cap and a shot through the after-funnel and one on the quarter-deck. The *Swiftsure's* Ward-room was wrecked, and she was struck twice forward and once amidships. Casualties—one man slightly wounded!

Gradually the two ships lengthened their range, and very late in the evening we went to their assistance. The fore-turret fired six rounds and the after-turret two. The first two shots from the fore-turret fell short; but with the third we got the range, and the fourth fell right in the fort, and it ceased fire. The range was 12,500 yards, and in the fading light the fort was hard to see. The *Canopus* made a signal to us: "Manœuvre well executed"—that was to say, "Well done."

For a short spell we had a watch off from

## THE PRELIMINARY LANDINGS

bombarding, and worked hard instead at taking in ammunition and stores. Rumour was busy—most of our rumours originated in hospital ships—with a yarn about a large army of English and French troops who were coming to back up our efforts; but recollecting those ubiquitous Russians who tiptoed through England in the night, we kept an open mind on the subject. At the moment we had with us three troopers with a Brigade of Marines, who later took part in so much of the fighting on the Peninsula. A second rumour—we ought not to number them, they were so many—told us that the Turkish fleet had sailed from Constantinople. That might be. We had seen two or three ships at Chanak, under the guns of the Narrows forts.

Our longest job of work was on March 4th, when we were at "Action Stations" from 10 a.m. to 7 p.m. On that day 250 men of the Royal Marines in the *Braemar Castle* were detailed for a landing at Kum Kale, when it was hoped to utterly destroy Fort 4. A similar party was to demolish anything left in the Sedd-ul-Bahr position. All the ships present sent picket-boats, cutters, and launches to disembark the troops, and the duty of the *Cornwallis* was to cover the Mendere River side of Kum Kale.

The earthworks of Kum Kale fort ran out into a promontory, and between them and the sea was a narrow strip of flat sand, which, as one followed it along the western shore, broadened out into a wide beach, on which stood in picturesque idleness two of the windmills of the country. Behind the beach lay the first houses of the village. Eastward a trestle pier jutted into the sea, and the thin riband of sand widened into a foreshore, which continued for a mile and a half, until it was brought up short by the forbidding cliffs on which the village of Yeni Shehir perched rakishly.

The boats were not far from the *Brœmar Castle* when they were fired upon from the western end of the ridge. Kum Kale village was full of snipers, and Fort 4 occupied by Turkish infantry. Extraordinary as it sounds, though there were many narrow escapes during the actual drawing up to the landing-places, there were no casualties; but in an attempt to land at the trestle pier, out of four patrols of five men each which got ashore only five men survived. The entire length

## THE PRELIMINARY LANDINGS

of the pier was under the fire of Turkish snipers concealed in the houses.

After the débâcle at the pier, a landing was effected at the end of the earthworks on the narrow strip of sand, and from the covering parapet of a bank the attack developed along the beach in the direction of Fort 4, opposite to which our men were presently able to advance a little; but never during the whole day did we hold any appreciable amount of land other than the shore. The snipers in the houses controlled the whole of the positions our men had to cross.

Here, again, was the dark shadow of the ammunition shortage. The necessity for economy prevented the artillery preparation vital for such a landing, and for the first time in these operations we experienced the stubbornness and skill with which the Turks can hold fortified places.

The tide was out when the expedition got ashore, and by keeping close to the water behind the sandy ridge the men got a certain amount of cover; but when the tide came up in the evening the slight elevation which had afforded some shelter in the morning disappeared, and to this was due much of the loss in the retirement which commenced in the evening, when it was realized that no further advance was possible. The retreat was of course the signal for the enemy to progress, and out he came in considerable force.

In this Calvary of courage every man had to run the gauntlet of the last twenty or thirty yards of the exposed beach. Some crawled on their hands and knees with the water up to their necks and bullets raining around. Many were killed, some were wounded, and it was dark before the last man was taken off.

On the pier lay the bodies of those gallants who fell early in the fight. Four maxims had been abandoned there by us in the disastrous landing, and during the day one of these was recovered by a marine, who dashed down the pier regardless of the phut! phut! of many bullets. He brought the gun back on his shoulder. The other three were retrieved by a volunteer cutter's crew.

From where we were we could see the Turks sheltering behind Fort 4, and as we had a clear target on masses of the enemy we opened fire, enfilading them. It was a glorious sight to see our shell scatter them, and we got in a number—we could see the shell-burst knocking them over,

# THE PRELIMINARY LANDINGS

and in the midst of it the Admiral sent us an encouraging signal: "Good shooting on Fort 4. You seem to be shaking the Turks."

When the Turks ran to cover in the buildings at the back, we put several lyddite shell slap into their shelters. Most of the time we were under a hot fire ourselves, and many shots dropped uncomfortably close, over or short. One just missed the stern and burst on striking the water, fragments hitting the stern-walk.

As the last of the landing party straggled down to the beach, and the Turks were momentarily expected to rush the end of the earthworks in the dusk, orders were given to our waiting picket-boat and cutter to open fire with maxims. Here, again, was the assurance that the watchful Providence which has at all times held the *Cornwallis* in mind was at His post.

The maxims in both boats jambed. And it was suddenly realized that the men on whom they would have been turned were our own!

To cover the retirement we fired strongly on Kum Kale village and started a big blaze.

We know something now of the difficulties with which the joint operations of sea and land are encompassed. During this most regrettable day, in which we lost some forty killed and sixty wounded, the signalling between the two forces was incomplete, and we never knew what part, if any, of the village was occupied by our men and what by the enemy.

After dark, boats from destroyers went in and collected from the beach all the wounded they could pick up—fifteen or thereabouts.

The landing at Sedd-ul-Bahr was successful, but we had no time to pay any attention to it. A story reached us of a sergeant of marines who fell in the first landing from the *Vengeance*, wounded in the legs only. Later, when a party of marines went to rescue him, they found his body full of bayonet wounds. A German caught near by was put up against a wall promptly.

The following day we and the *Irresistible* and the *Canopus* entered the Straits, and spotted the fall of shot for the *Queen Elizabeth* as she fired from the Ægean Sea, over a neck of land, at a range of 15,000 yards, at the forts in the Narrows. The result of the fall of each shot, which dropped every five or ten minutes into or around the forts and continued for about four hours, was signalled by wireless telegraphy—a most interesting example of modern gunnery. The *Queen*

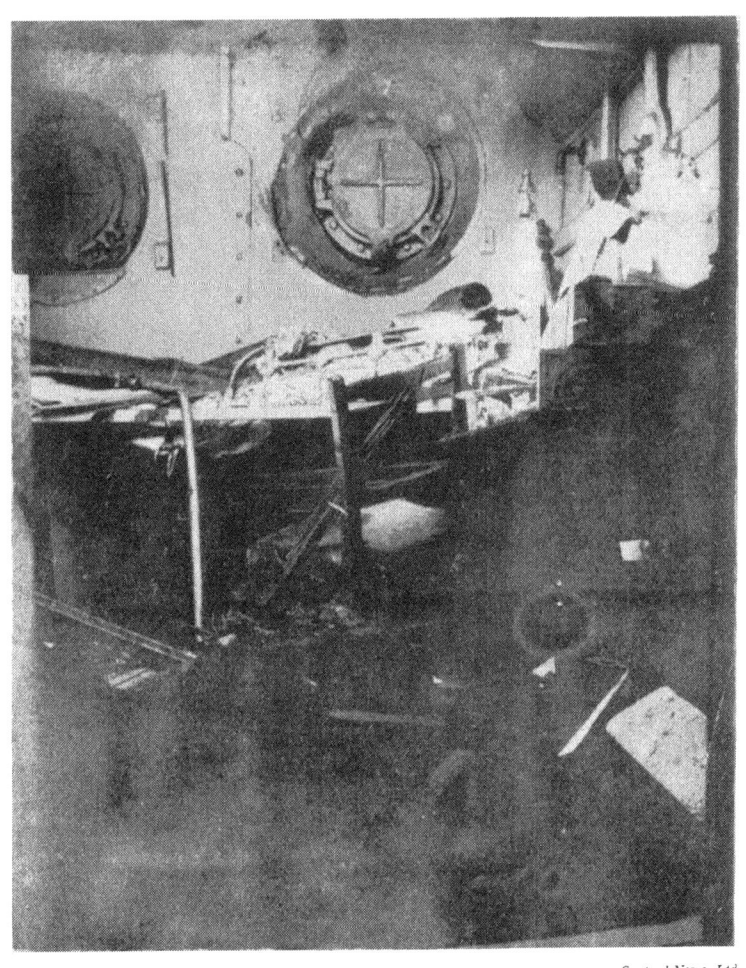

*Central News, Ltd*

OFFICER'S CABIN WRECKED BY A SHELL *page* 44).

FORT 6, KUM KALE, TO WHICH A TOW OF BOATS WAS BEIN

MINE-SWEEPING TRAWLERS CARRYING OUT THEIR FIRST SWEEP AT THE ENTRANCE TO THE DARDANELLES ON THE EVENING OF FEBRUARY 26, 1915.

AKEN WHEN THIS PHOTOGRAPH WAS OBTAINED UNDER FIRE.

THE DESTRUCTION OF KUM KALE. WAKE OF THE "CORNWALLIS" IS SEEN.

PREPARING TO LAND 2ND BATTALION SOUTH WALES BORDERERS ON APRIL 25, 1915 (*page* 74).

*Elizabeth* appeared to get a good proportion of hits, and one shot we thought reached a magazine, as there was an unusually heavy explosion.

The Narrows forts opened fire on us, but could not reach us, although a few shells dropped fairly close and whistled unpleasantly near the tops. Howitzers on the near ridges engaged us at intervals, and we silenced them again and again. It was their way to stop firing as soon as we got the range. Some of our shells reached them all right. Over by Kum Kale the French mine-sweepers were doing excellent work under a heavy fire.

Sometimes o' nights the Ward-room tried to analyze the sensation of being under fire—it defies pulling to pieces almost. Certainly it is soul-shaking. You have seen the flash, and then there is the breathless wait . . . a whistle rises *en crescendo* to a subdued shriek that ends with a dull double clap like a heavy weight falling on a deck. You wonder vaguely where on earth it will fall, and when, as sometimes, two or three shells come along together, your cup of anxiety flows over. One could never become utterly callous to it— there is too much of the last moment about it for that. The fellow who described this war as "months of weary waiting punctuated by moments of intense fear" was right.

On the 8th March we were one of the covering ships for the *Queen Elizabeth* within the Straits as she bombarded Fort 13 at the Narrows. Our duty was to keep in check the local batteries, and each of the ships was accompanied by a picket-boat steaming ahead looking for mines.

The *Irresistible* reported a find, and her picket-boat sank two of our floating enemies, the ricochets from her 3-pounder coming very close to our foretop.

Again our luck held, and though we were repeatedly straddled, and shells fell a yard ahead and close astern — Fort 13 was making most excellent practice with heavy guns — we were not hit. The light was bad for spotting, and the *Queen Elizabeth* only fired a few shots. She was not there to be knocked about, and retired out of range when the enemy opened fire. This time we had some 6-inch shrapnel, and after trying to hit a big howitzer which ran on rails for half a mile or so at the foot of Aren Keui village, we got the range, and gave them some splendid salvoes, winding up with a few rounds of lyddite.

Standing for hours searching the hillsides for

likely objects, trying to spot the smoke and flashes of enemy guns, one got weary of holding the glasses to one's eyes. Well, there was no use worrying because we did not progress very fast! And every day we told ourselves we had bagged some Turks, and we always hoped that among them were a good few Germans.

We were as high up the Straits on this day of chaperoning the *Queen Elizabeth* as any ship had been. If only we had had sea room instead of being in a narrow waterway! Ordinary forts cannot stand against long-range bombardment by moving ships.

It was our way to call many of these places of our bombardings "villages," but you would not always find them on the map—at least, by the names we gave them; often they were a mere huddle of shaly débris, terraced with a certain rough cultivation on bastions which seemed as if everything had slid together like a child's Noah's ark overturned. So many days we had of studying the place that every detail came out before we had finished with it as if within pistol shot. And because it was a new thing, so little like the numbing routine of ship life, with its meals at regular hours, its familiar responsibilities, its interruptions, even its pleasures, we much preferred the hard days of action and danger to our brief rests (so-called) in Mudros.

March 10th provided a dull afternoon for us in the Gulf of Xeros shelling the lines and village of Bulair—a muggy, thick day, and the light could not have been worse. The enemy made no reply, and we were glad to get back to our patrol off the Dardanelles. During the next two nights the firing within the Straits was incessant. The trawlers were making heroic efforts to clear up the mines.

On the evening of the 13th March—" there is divinity in odd numbers either in nativity, chance, or death "—the *Cornwallis* set forth on " an awfully big adventure." We were to try and attack and put out of action the searchlights which shone out on the Asiatic side from Kephez Point at Fort 8 and those near Fort 7, preparatory to a carefully planned attempt to clear the minefields in readiness for a great effort which it was known the fleet was to make to force the Narrows.

Far, far outside the Straits the rays of the searchlights seemed to be playing on us, exposing us who would be hidden. It was fancy

## THE PRELIMINARY LANDINGS 37

really; the friendly darkness concealed our machinations, the very wind, blowing off the land, muffled our progress. It was a most uncanny experience—the big ghostly ship moving forward towards the brilliant eyes. Nearer and nearer we crept, and at 8,000 yards they discovered us, almost with an "Hurrah!" could searchlights but voice their feelings, and six of them pounced on us and turned our night to day. We opened fire at once then, but it was impossible to spot the shots, and if we extinguished one light or it extinguished itself, another was switched on in its stead.

We ourselves could see nothing, and the velvety darkness around was intensified a hundred times by the vivid lights playing on us, searching us up and down. One felt then our every movement was seen by the enemy. In reality our danger was much less than by day.

Repeatedly Fort 13 fired heavy shells at us, and their rush and roar was like the sound of an express train. We were probably saved from being hit by going full speed astern, which threw out the enemy ranges, and we retired outside the Straits in our own time when the "Secure" was sounded.

The sweepers and picket-boats, supported by the *Amethyst* and T.B.D.'s, then entered with the object of steaming right through the minefield until they reached Chanak, when they would turn, connect sweeps, and come back through the minefield. During this manœuvre we were under strict orders on no account to go into the Straits, as it was thought that on previous occasions the battleships had given away the position of the trawlers.

Our trawlers worked in pairs, connected one with the other by their sweeping gear. The picket-boats had grappling-irons, known as "creeps," which they let down to the estimated depth of the minefield, a method which proved most useful in the Dardanelles, where the mines were laid in trots. The French sweepers worked singly, with a cutting arrangement in the sweep. The mines, when caught by the creeps, were exploded by means of an electric spark,* or else the tearing of the trot set the mines free to float down on the current, when it was simple enough to locate and destroy them.

* These explosive creeps are grapnels fitted with small gun-cotton charges fired by a battery in the boat when the creep holds.

## THE PRELIMINARY LANDINGS 39

The adventures of No. 1 picket-boat on this hazardous adventure were related to us by Midshipman Last. "The trawlers," he said, "were to go in line ahead followed by the picket-boats, and when up as far beyond Kephez Point as possible, keeping close to the European shore, to pair off, get out sweeps, and sweep downstream in quarter-line to port, each pair slightly overlapping the next ahead. The picket-boats were to go beyond Kephez Point, turn round, get out creeps, blow up anything caught, then return upstream and try again with a second creep. It was a perfectly still, clear night, cold and very dark. There were three searchlights showing—one throwing a steady beam across the Straits from Fort 7, and two others at Chanak and Kilid Bahr (one a large reddish light and the other a very large white one), which searched the surface of the water from Asia to Europe.

"Before they were discovered the trawlers had passed Fort 7, which presently opened a heavy though rather inaccurate fire, as did the fort at the Narrows and many guns on the European shore. Two more medium-power searchlights were switched on, and on seeing this the picket-boats, abandoning their original formation, went full speed ahead to catch up with the trawlers. Passing Fort 7, the picket-boats were greeted with shrapnel and common, and the shots from the Narrows, which missed the trawlers, came nearer to us than those specially hall-marked for us by Fort 7.

"Close to the Narrows the trawlers bunched in attempting to get out their sweeps, and came under an accurate fire. Meanwhile the picket-boats turned and got out their creeps. Ours caught something good and hard almost at once, and we fired it, turning upstream for a second effort. Five of the trawlers were coming down at full speed, having been prevented by casualties from getting out their sweeps at all. Only one pair had any success, and close in to the European shore they were sweeping methodically. We had barely got our second creep down—a lucky cast—when the flag picket-boat came up and told us to clear out."

All the firing had been heard by us in the *Cornwallis*, lying outside the Straits, and at about four o'clock in the morning we went inside the entrance until we were perhaps 8,000 yards from Fort 7, when we stopped engines. Four trawlers were coming down the Straits, and

THE PRELIMINARY LANDINGS 41

the *Amethyst*, floating like a wounded sea-bird, was making a signal: " Am in great need of medical help. Send as many cots as possible." Instantly Surgeon Irvine, with sick-berth stewards, cots, and first-aid appliances, went off to her assistance.

The light cruiser had experienced a terrible time. Having got up as far as Fort 7 in support of the sweepers her steering gear was disabled, her bridge-to-engine-room communication destroyed, and her lights put out by the first shots. For twenty minutes she lay out of control in the glare of the searchlights, exposed to the fire of guns of all sizes. Hand-steering gear was rigged, and she came out of the danger zone, after being struck twelve times, with 22 killed, 28 severely wounded, and 10 slightly wounded. The greatest loss was caused by a shot which went into the stokers' bathroom and killed and mangled one watch of stokers. Another shot did much the same thing in the foc'sle mess-deck.

The T.B.D. *Mosquito* came alongside signalling for medical help, and our second Surgeon, Galloway, went to her. He found on board four men from one of the trawlers in which every man had been killed or wounded, and these four were transferred to us.

The dawn was just breaking, and the sun, rising in splendour, touched with warm glory the dull-toned Peninsula and the far, faint misty hills rising here and there beyond Chanak. Gliding and glowing in the grey channels of the shore a thousand beams turned all the hueless things to gold, and in the stead of them was a vast lagoon of bright, shadowless water.

Dawn and death hand in hand—it was an irony such as only a D'Annunzio would appreciate and plain seamen like ourselves pass by as all in war's work.

There was so little left of the first of the wounded to bring in-board at all—a broken trunk of a man with both legs shot away by a shell and an indomitable courage that flickered out just as we hoisted the ensign at 8 bells.

The Vice-Admiral commended the conduct of all concerned in the operations, which had maintained, he said, "the best traditions of our Service"; and whilst regretting the loss of life, he explained that good work had been done, as many mines were destroyed.

Late in the afternoon—March 14th—we went

## THE PRELIMINARY LANDINGS 43

to "Action Stations," and prepared to bombard Fort 7. Until we reached a bluff west of the Suan Dere River, we kept to the European shore, and then steamed more into the middle of the Straits. Opening fire on the surmised position of Fort 7, our shots were quickly returned by batteries on the bluff, followed by others still farther west and by a heavy battery of four guns lying inland behind a ridge of hills. This last made excellent practice; every shot fell close to us, and at last they landed one on our quarter-deck, abaft the screen door between the after-turret and the X.I casemate. Fortunately, it did no damage except to break through the upper deck and wreck the P.M.O.'s cabin beneath. The after-screen was pierced in several places, and the 12-inch and the 6-inch guns were scored by splinters. The protected deck was not touched, and altogether it was an interesting illustration of how much strain of plunging fire the decks would stand. It was also important to have located this battery, which had not been done previously, as it had made good shooting for days past on every ship working on this particular bearing.

In and out of the P.M.O.'s ruinous cabin

souvenir hunters roamed, delving assiduously for bits of shell. It had a most extraordinary attraction for the men, who could not keep away, and the P.M.O. complained very bitterly. A few days later, as he was censoring letters, he came across a glowing account of the wreckage of the cabin. The writer bewailed the fact that he had not managed to arrive on the scene in time to pick up a piece of shell as a souvenir. " But, never mind," he added; " I got the doctor's pipe."

A fruitless search in Morto Bay for mines finished our day's work, and for a change we were sniped at by rifle fire from the shore, one bit of flattened bullet falling into the foretop.

# CHAPTER III

### THE BATTLE OF THE NARROWS

A DEMONSTRATION off Gaba Tepe, which drew no reply from the shore, brought us up to March 17th, the day before the big attack on the Narrows, which, for various political reasons, as we understood the case, was to be made. The Captain went to the flagship to receive final orders, and general disappointment reigned when he told us that the *Cornwallis*, with the *Canopus*, was to remain in reserve outside the Straits. His orders were to enter after the main attack had taken place, and to act as guard to the mine-sweepers at night. The *Ocean* was originally told off for this, but as she and the *Canopus* were commanded by senior Captains, the *Cornwallis* was ordered to change places with the *Ocean*, and thereby the first of our providential escapes from being sunk was ensured.

"A mighty big affair and full of difficulties," as one of our strategists on the lower deck described the imminent attack, it was rendered extraordinarily embarrassing by the confined space in which we had to work. Had the Straits been ten miles wide we should have been in Constantinople long ago. The mines were the real things to fear; we outclassed the Turkish gunnery at all times. They could only hit the ships when they were stopped.

Our newspapers from home were filled with optimistic accounts of the Dardanelles operations. We were performing miracles every day and twice on Sundays—a wonderful list of occurrences described by those to whom they were related by others who did not see them. As for the photographs of ships and incidents, any old name served. If there is a humorous side to this ghastly war, one finds it in some of the cheaper illustrated papers, whose idea of the public intelligence is plainly indicated. One can imagine the editor saying to himself; " Now I wonder if they'll swallow *this* !" as he christens the portrait of an oyster-shell, appropriately capped and moustached, " General Sarrail," and " Joffre's favourite charger " one week, " the last cow left alive by the Huns in Belgium " the next.

THE BATTLE OF THE NARROWS 47

In the forenoon of March 17th a signal was received that E.15 had run aground off Kephez, and that her officers and crew were prisoners of the Turks. She was going up above Chanak to attempt to destroy a Turkish battleship reported to be there by our aeroplanes.

From the first there was little hope of getting the submarine off, and every effort was made to destroy her before the enemy could make use of her. First the aeroplanes tried to drop bombs on her, and when this scheme failed two T.B.D.'s went up to torpedo her, but did not succeed. One of the B. submarines made a great effort to put a torpedo into her, but only managed to sink a tug which was alongside. The *Triumph* tried the effect of shell fire, but little or no damage was done.

It was not until Lieutenant-Commander Robinson went up with two picket-boats, one of which was sunk in the attempt, that from their dropping gear E.15 was torpedoed. The story of this attack, carried out at night under heavy fire, is one of the most thrilling occurrences of all the wonderful happenings at the Dardanelles, and ranks with any of the historical cutting-out exploits of the Old Navy.

The plan of the attack on the Narrows was as follows: At 8.30 a.m. on the fatal March 18th the first division left Tenedos. Our band played them out of harbour. The other two divisions followed about 10.30.

We could see nothing of the preliminary firing or its effect, and our only information came from the wireless signals of the aeroplanes, whose constant reports told of the manning and efficiency of the forts, their fire, and the fall of our shell. It was not until the action was over that we heard how the day had gone for us.

After leaving Tenedos, the four long-range ships entered the Straits and opened fire on the forts in the Narrows at a range of 14,000 yards, and this bombardment was continued for an hour and a half. Then the French ships passed through the first division and engaged the forts at about 10,000 yards, sustaining a terrific fire, until they began to retire and the third division relieved them.

It was at this time the *Bouvet* was blown up, and sank in less than three minutes with nearly all hands, only five officers and fifty-six men being saved out of the ship's company of over eight hundred.

## THE BATTLE OF THE NARROWS 49

The third division, undaunted, went within a range of 9,000 yards on a line drawn from Suan Dere River and Kephez Point, and sank the only thing they could see afloat — a small two-masted one-funnel steamer off Suan Dere.

The forts had the range fairly soon, and the *Irresistible* and the *Ocean* suffered considerably — the *Irresistible* especially, and before long both her turrets were out of action, and in addition to the rest of her troubles she grounded off Kephez Point under Fort 8, known on the map as Dardanus. The *Ocean* had her signalling apparatus, including wireless and searchlights, shot away, and at about 4 o'clock she received orders to take the *Irresistible* in tow. The latter was in a bad way. Salvo after salvo of shots were poured into her. As someone described the scene: "It was like a gigantic shovel throwing huge lumps of coal on a flameless fire from which belched out thick black smoke."

As the *Ocean* cautiously felt her way across the Straits, she hoisted in a boatload of wounded coming down from the *Irresistible*, and close to that battered ship went aground herself, only getting off by going full speed astern.

To tow off the *Irresistible* * was impossible, and the *Ocean* returned to her attack on the forts, and at about 5.30 p.m. it was noticed that the fire from the land batteries was slacking; indeed, some officers and men are convinced that in one of them a white flag was raised.

Shortly after this the *Ocean* was struck by a mine or torpedo fired from the mouth of the Suan Dere River. Opinion is divided equally as to which it was, but everything points to the weapon of destruction being a torpedo.

The ship listed to starboard, and the shock of the explosion jammed her steering gear. The helm being hard-a-port turned the ship right round, and she went aground, heading up the Dardanelles. At once the T.B.D.'s *Chelmer* and *Kennet* came alongside, and under a heavy fire removed everyone from the *Ocean*. The *Chelmer* was so badly hit herself that her Captain signalled the *Kennet* to stand by, and the *Kennet* replied they were making water in the engine-room. Temporary repairs, however, kept both

* Naval opinion is undecided whether the *Irresistible* was aground or in a backwater with engine-room flooded. A destroyer going in to torpedo the abandoned battleship at 1 a.m. on the morning following found no *Irresistible* to torpedo.

## THE BATTLE OF THE NARROWS

going, and as they proceeded down the Straits with their decks crowded, a signal was made for the men of the *Ocean* to rejoin their ship, an order impossible to obey, as the stricken battleship was sinking lower and lower in the water. At 8.10 she disappeared.

As the *Kennet*, with part of the *Ocean's* crew, returned up the Dardanelles, a strong swimmer was seen coming down with the current. The *Kennet* stopped and picked him up.

"I was just swimming down to Tenedos," he said—Tenedos being twenty miles away!—" to tell you that you've left four men in the *Ocean*."

The destroyer pushed ahead with all speed, and sure enough there were four forlorn stokers sitting on the foc'sle, which was just awash.

At 2 o'clock in the afternoon the *Cornwallis* weighed and left Tenedos with the *Canopus* for the entrance of the Straits, and both remained outside according to orders. Within, a terrific bombardment was going on, the forts, batteries, and our own ships firing. The *Agamemnon* was noticeable as being surrounded by falling shells, but all the ships were heavily fired upon.

Looking back at it—one is always so preternaturally wise afterwards—it is remarkable that more damage was not done to the ships and that the loss of life was no heavier. An artillery expert who was on board the *Queen Elizabeth* expressed the opinion that, from his experience of shooting from forts protecting harbours, no ship ought to have come out of the Dardanelles, with, perhaps, the exception of the *Queen Elizabeth*.

At about 4 p.m. the *Gaulois*, down by the head, came out of the straits steaming very, very slowly, surrounded by destroyers and convoyed by the *Suffren*, which kept astern. We called away all boats, as did the *Canopus*, and sent them to stand by.

Then followed the most exciting three-quarters of an hour—it was touch and go whether the great ship could reach Rabbit Island and beach herself.

Deeper and deeper she sank, slower and slower she steamed; her stern was cocked up and her bows down to the anchor flukes.

As she floated away, a vast bulk led off between the little craft, the massive battleship reminded one of a wild elephant, roped and helpless for all her power, in the custody of inferior beasts, civilized into subserviency.

THE BATTLE OF THE NARROWS 53

In the midst of this struggle for existence the *Inflexible* was seen leaving the entrance, and a sudden call was made for destroyers to go to her. She, too, was down at the bows, and all hands were gathered aft, but we were relieved to see that she could steam at a fast rate. A big hole was reported forward in her, and presently she made the reassuring signal to the Commander-in-Chief: " Hope to be able to reach Tenedos." This, thank God, she managed to do.

And the *Gaulois*, scarce moving, crept towards Rabbit Island, where she beached herself just in time, for the bulkhead gave way as the ship came to rest.

\*     \*     \*     \*     \*

It was 9.30 before the fleet left the Straits, after a very unsatisfactory day for us—the *Bouvet*, *Irresistible*, and *Ocean* lost, the *Gaulois* and *Inflexible* damaged.

The anchors of the *Gaulois* were jammed, and we sent our stream anchor across with the First-Lieutenant, together with our carpenters and divers, one of whom described the Admiral of the French fleet, who was alongside the *Gaulois*, as "a fine, upright, and polite gentleman, with clear eyes, white moustache, and beard."

He was, of course, Admiral Guépratte. He shook hands with all the *Cornwallis* men, and thanked them for their prompt and efficient help.

A striking feature of the day was the curious fact that the floating mines of the enemy were not effective until some hours after the first shot of the bombardment had been fired. No tide runs into the Dardanelles, and the outgoing current varies in strength from two to five knots, according to the wind. One of the strongest defences of the Narrows, therefore, was the opportunity which the outgoing current afforded of letting loose floating mines. Naval men for many days afterwards argued the question as to whether, at any period of the operations, a dash through the Narrows was possible, and naturally enough the 18th March was cited as one of the rare occasions on which the attempt might have been successful. The concensus of opinion seemed to be that no dash would have prospered except after the demoralizing effect of the bombardment of the outer forts on February 26th. Had it been feasible to have passed on

## THE BATTLE OF THE NARROWS

to the bombardment of the forts at the Narrows immediately with the expenditure of unlimited ammunition, we might have got through into the Sea of Marmora. But it must always be borne in mind that the enemy had two great forces in their hands—their minefields and their forts. The one acted as a defence for the other. Whilst the minefields were efficient, the forts could not be approached; and whilst the forts remained intact, the minefields could not be swept.

Now at last we hoped the newspapers and the people at home would begin to take a reasonable view of our difficulties, and would cease making nothing of the forces with which we had to deal.

We had our turn of patrols and coaled religiously every three or four days, and the myriad little incidents that went to make up our daily lives crowded in on us.

One hundred and fifteen ratings of the lost *Irresistible* suddenly arrived without any warning, and 115 unexpected visitors is rather a handful in the best regulated ship's company. Our mess-decks were crowded before they came, but we welcomed the shipwrecked as warmly as we could. Spare winter clothing was served out to them, ship's clothing as well. From these men we gathered something of the scene aboard the *Irresistible* ere she was abandoned. The main losses apparently were caused by the shrapnel sweeping the quarter-deck. The port engine-room was blown up, and only one man escaped from it—the rush of water forced him through a hatchway.

And on the loss of our ships on the memorable 18th March hangs a tale too good to leave untold. Among the shipwrecked was a Lieutenant who had been the joy of successive messmates for years. Thackeray would have loved him and awarded him a special niche in the "Book of Snobs."

By hailing them all as cousins and uncles and aunts, the blue-blooded Lieutenant has related the entire peerage to one another. Occasionally he makes a mistake, and claims some blatant *nouveau riche* disguised under a high-sounding title, a mistake he skims over in his own airy, lightsome fashion by pretending he never made it.

Since he left the *Britannia* a huge "Family Tree" has accompanied him in all his wanderings, and however small his cabin the papyrus roll is extended from deck to deck, all in readiness for him to show you artlessly, and in what he thinks a natural way, the leaf which sustains his name. Tradition has it that during a refit a dockyard "matey" working outside the cabin was shown the "Family Tree." The "matey" liked it, he liked it very much. "It be a rare fine picture, sir," he said contemplatively; "I fancies them little leaves standing up so imperent looking. I've a mind to get a picture like it for myself. Where d'you buy them, sir?"

To the Russian moujik his sacred icon ranks above all other of his possessions. "If your house takes fire, save the icon and samovar first, and then, if you have time, the children," is an old saying. Something of this idea was in our minds as we all bet upon what the Lieutenant would save first in the event of his ship being lost. We all won. Sure enough, at the last moment, as everyone was leaving the sinking battleship, the illustrious one bethought himself of what he was leaving behind. All the hatches in the after-part being closed, he found a broken skylight, through which he nipped, and reaching his cabin, he salved the genealogical tree.

This is a true story, for it is the Lieutenant's own.

An unexpected treat for us was the weighing of the anchors and twenty shackles of cable belonging to the *Inflexible*, which she had been obliged to slip off Tenedos owing to a shift of wind. They were badly fouled, and took a day and a half to weigh.

A Turkish aeroplane—they had just obtained a few from somewhere, and were as proud of them as a little boy with a new kite—provided an interlude in the shape of an attack on the *Ark Royal*—a near thing for the latter.

The *Ark Royal*, the aviation headquarters ship, made a partner in quaintness for the odd-looking French *Henri IV.*, which joined the fleet after the loss of the *Bouvet*, and which, viewed from astern, with her curiously built up turrets on turrets rising in high tiers from a low freeboard, reminded one of nothing so much as some ancient Welsh castle—Harlech, perhaps, or Carnarvon—broken loose.

During one of our cruises off the coast, Bunting, a recently promoted petty officer, fell overboard from the boat-deck. Surgeon Galloway, walking on the quarter-deck, saw Bunting, who was not a good swimmer, struggling in a very choppy sea, and jumped after him — a high dive and no mistake! Meanwhile Engineer Lieutenant-Commander Cooke unlashed a buoy and threw it into the water, and almost as it touched, Petty Officer Jarvis, seeing that Dr. Galloway would have his work cut out to save Bunting, followed. Between the two of them Bunting was all right, and our cutter picked up the three, none the worse for the adventure.

Both Dr. Galloway and Petty Officer Jarvis received the Royal Humane Society's certificate, though we had hoped and thought a medal each would have been awarded.

## CHAPTER IV

### STEPPING-STONES

VERY often letters from home would ask us how it was that the islands we used as anchoring places and bases could be adapted to our needs without infringing somebody's neutrality, and, like so many questions of a similar nature, the query had to go unanswered.

After the Græco-Turkish War of 1912, the Greeks took the island of Lemnos—(quite a biggish island as they go in the Ægean), together with the smaller islands, from the Turks; and when peace was signed the question of ownership was left for an after-settlement, which never materialized, with the result that both countries claimed them. This state of affairs enabled the Allies, warring against Turkey, to make use of the Turkish half at least without infringing Greek neutrality; and directly a base was required for the army gathering for the great

STEPPING-STONES 61

landing, the harbour of Mudros, which practically cuts the island of Lemnos in two, was selected as being large enough to hold all the ships, naval and mercantile, which would be utilized.

Lemnos, with Kastro its capital, lies in a westerly direction from the entrance to the Straits. A little necklace of islands surrounded us on every side—just such romantic places as poets write about and take good care not to live in.

It was in Mudros we first realized that the rumoured army which was to clear the Peninsula and open up for us the way through the Narrows was something more than the usual camera-obscura magnifier. From a moderate-sized village with a few primitive shops of the general store variety the place had suddenly become the gathering-ground of the vultures who collect on the outskirts of all armies. Both sides of the road leading from the pier were covered with the booths of hucksters selling all manner of foodstuffs, cheap trinkets, wines and fiery spirits. Here was a medley of people and the tongue of many lands.

Beyond a business-like Australian hospital unit

was an Australian camp, and the transports coming into harbour were full of the men from overseas, who landed a battalion at a time, practising as they came ashore the tactics they expected to follow in actual warfare. They struck us as being as fine a body of men physically as one could meet in a summer's day, and their clothing and accoutrements were of the best. They came to Mudros from Egypt, with the reputation of having painted Cairo very red (and in colour-blind Cairo this is something of an achievement), and were to prove in the Peninsula that no finer natural fighters exist.

Under the hills to the west of the village was a camp of French soldiers, whose blue uniforms touched with red were a contrast in colour schemes to the dull-hued khaki of our men. To add to the staginess of the whole scene—if you shut your eyes for a second you could transport yourself to the first act of a successful musical comedy at home—Senegalese troops direct from West Africa were shaking down alongside a battalion of Zouaves. The Senegalese were thick-set, smart-looking men of moderate height, and every one of them had a skin black as ebony. They were punctilious in saluting all officers, and

STEPPING-STONES 63

had the reputation of being excellent in hand-to-hand fights.

For the next few days the gunnery department of the ship was busy decoppering the 6-inch guns, as the constant firing had left a metal residue which choked the rifling and would cause inaccuracy if not removed.

Mudros was filling up, and every day there were arrivals of half a dozen transports at least, which were secured together in pairs to save space in the harbour. Gradually we came to understand that we were on the eve of the biggest combined expedition on record, and that unfolded before our eyes was the mightiest spectacle, the most dazzling psychological scenario, that had ever been seen on any stage.

The ships were so many they could not be counted, but there must have been a hundred and sixty other than men-of-war and small craft in the harbour—ships of the Cunard, R.M.S.P. Company, Bucknall, P. & O., American, A.V.S.N., New Zealand Shipping Company, Bibby, W.A.S.N. Company, Atlantic Transport, Isle of Man Steampacket Company, Rennie, G.S.N. Company, Allan, Leyland, B.I., China Merchant, Bullard and King, C.P.R., and Shire lines; the

French M.M., M.M.T., and Algiers to Marseilles Mail lines. The Hambourg-American was represented by a goodly prize. In the outer anchorage at least forty large ships lay, including French transports, noticeable for the beauty of their design, low in the water and lean-looking as compared with the appearance of the built-up, top-heavy Cunarders.

Saturday, the 3rd April, we were to have gone on patrol, but our gun cleaning was not completed. In the late afternoon our Chaplain went out in some small craft to bury the remains of a boy from the *Inflexible*, her Captain, Chaplain, and firing-party going also, and from them the padre gathered something of what happened on the 18th March.

The first shell, which struck their foretop, killed two men and wounded the Gunnery-Commander and a Lieutenant, and almost immediately a second shell hit the ladder leg of the tripod mast and set it on fire. No help could be sent to the foretop for half an hour, owing to the flames spreading upwards; but at last the two officers, who died later in the hospital ship *Soudan*, were rescued. Shortly afterwards the *Inflexible* struck a mine, which cost her twenty-nine men blown up and drowned in the fore torpedo-flat. Eventually she managed to reach Malta under her own steam, after a coffer-dam had been built over the damaged part of the side and the hole patched. This Dreadnought cruiser is known to the most ignorant of the general public—and it must be conceded that the general public knows very little of the navy of which it is so proud—as one of the squadron which put an end to Von Spee off the Falkland Isles.

April 6th saw us patrolling the entrance of the Dardanelles with the *Implacable,* and on the day following we went up the Straits for one and a half miles, the distance reported by the mine-sweepers as having been cleared. We gave greeting to our old friends at the southern end of the Aren Keui ridge, and they returned it gracefully—a dozen rounds, and all wide. We also sent four 6-inch into Aren Keui village and three 6-inch into Kum Kale, as they were heliographing from both places. In the evening as it grew dark we fired a few rounds at a searchlight behind Sedd-ul-Bahr without affecting it in the least. The searchlight still searched.

Just about this time, when the *Cornwallis* was on patrol, ambling along at six knots, a destroyer in the distance suddenly opened fire on the land.

" Full speed ahead " rang down from the bridge, and off we dashed and closed with the destroyer, signalling as we did so from Captain to Captain:

" Please inform me what you are firing at."

At once the laconic reply came back:

" A camel on the beach."

Sometimes when the wind came off the land, particularly at the close of a sultry day, a strong, virile scent blew upon us with messages from the Peninsula. It was indefinable, but there was dust in it, the hot odour of a multitude, sweat and things putrefying, hemp and oil, sour fruit and goats.

It was the smell of the East.

We practised landing troops from transports at Mudros, and gave them some training in getting ashore from boats to beaches, rehearsing all manner of evolutions in the face of a make-believe enemy, until we came near enough to the real thing to be told off with the *Euryalus* and *Implacable* as one organization for the gamble ahead.

As we lay in Mudros, sudden orders were received for the *Racoon* to raise steam. News had come through that a Turkish torpedo boat, which was known to have escaped down the Dardanelles to Smyrna, had come out and torpedoed the transport *Manitou*. Later we heard that the *Wear* and *Minerva* had cut off the T.B., and chased her until she was forced to beach herself. Rumour had it that over a hundred men in the *Manitou* were drowned in the first panic, and a mutilated signal suggested the loss of the ship. Great was the joy when the *Manitou* arrived and reported sixty men lost by jumping overboard, and not a hundred, as we had heard. An N.C.O. who had been present told us what had really happened. The Turkish T.B. was seen approaching, and, with some idea of playing the game, she actually gave the *Manitou* ten minutes to get her men into the boats. The transport had a gun on board, but it did not appear that there was any ammunition to hand or that any regular guns crews had been told off. Many soldiers did not wait for the boats, but jumped into the sea. The T.B. fired three torpedoes in succession from so close a range that the torpedoes after their first dive had not time to reach their fixed depth, and so passed clean under their prey.

68  THE IMMORTAL GAMBLE

During the next few days there was nothing doing so far as we were concerned. The landing of the army on the Peninsula loomed closer and closer, and fragmentary details became known to us. We gathered that the losses in prospect were to be heavy, and incidentally that we had been told off to cover a landing at Sedd-ul-Bahr, the *Euryalus* another farther north, and beyond that, again, the *Implacable* would be stationed. Lieutenant Morse was to be in charge of boats, and Lieutenant Budgen had already left the ship with a party to help in disembarking the army from the transports. Lieutenant Madge with a number of men would command the beach party from the *Cornwallis*, which was to land at Sedd-ul-Bahr beach. The Australians, we were told, would land at Gaba Tepe—far out of our beat; and the first aim of the invaders was to occupy the height of Achi Baba.

On April 21st the final council of Admirals and Captains was held on board the *Queen Elizabeth*. It was now only a matter of waiting for fine weather, and by Friday a rising barometer gave promise of favourable conditions. In company with the *Euryalus* and *Implacable* we left Mudros in the evening, our first move in the great attack.

We had a most stirring send-off from a Russian and a French man-of-war. Both gave us rounds of cheers, to which we replied with equal goodwill.

As we went out we had an opportunity of seeing the vastness of the mercantile fleet collected together, and few of us had seen a larger gathered in one spot.

The weather again changed. The wind got up, the barometer began to fall, and the moon rose with a windy, wet halo round it, which was decidedly unpromising, as we arrived at our old anchorage at Tenedos on the evening of April 24th. There was no further news for us, and we waited for fair weather.

That forenoon the Captain had addressed all hands on the quarter-deck. He told us that our first duty was to land seven hundred and fifty men of the 2nd Battalion of the South Wales Borderers at De Tott's Battery. They were a specially picked regiment, and the General had said that he would be satisfied if the soldiers took the ridge with a loss of 50 per cent. of their strength. Officers and men would come on board the night before that fixed for the landing, and it would be up to us not only to make them as comfortable as possible during their stay, but also to back them up to the best of our ability as they landed. General Hart, we were told, had wound up an address to his troops by saying: "With the help of God and the Navy, success will be ours."

In the afternoon orders were unexpectedly received to make ready at once for the South Wales Borderers—a great surprise, as all preparations for the landing had been postponed. They came to us in four trawlers from their transport, joining the ship at intervals during the evening, and the reputation they gained afterwards did not belie their appearance of extreme fitness. They already had some experience of war, having taken part in the siege and capture of Tsing-Tau.

The officers dined with us in the Ward-room, and the Captain entertained the Colonel. The men were made at home on the mess-deck, and whenever afterwards, as happened several times, the *Cornwallis* and the South Wales Borderers met, it was with mutual pleasure.

## CHAPTER V

#### THE GREAT LANDING

In all the history of our Empire there has been no feat such as April 25th, 1915, witnessed—the landing of troops in the face of trenches and slopes well protected and long prepared with every kind of device and death-dealing implement. As ciphers in the Immortal Gamble we may not comment on the breezy optimism of the military plans, which were surely based upon the assumption that no serious opposition was to be offered, otherwise they could not be carried into effect. That we had any success at all and gained any ground was due solely to the absolutely splendid pluck and determination of the soldiers, and the protection afforded by the guns of the navy.

Starting overnight from Tenedos anchorage, towing transports' life-boats, we steamed slowly towards the Gallipoli Peninsula. With us réveillé sounded at 3.30 a.m., and at 4.45 the trawlers came alongside and loaded up with our soldier guests—an expeditiously managed transference, for by 5 a.m. we were under weigh again ourselves.

It was a lovely morning, cold and windless, with a calm glassy sea, and presently the sun came up in a flood of gold—the last sunrise many of us were destined to look upon.

Ships were on every side—battleships and destroyers, transports and store-ships, trawlers and mine-sweepers, picket-boats and steam launches, with long snaky lines of cutters and life-boats in tow, and the now famous collier, the *River Clyde*.

Silently we steamed up the Straits in the grey light, and ahead of us crept the soldier-filled trawlers, until, passing the *Agamemnon* on the starboard hand, we anchored short of De Tott's Battery.

It appears to have been the general idea among the uninitiated at home, and by that we mean the non-readers of military history, the acceptors of ready-made tactics and strategy, that the landing of this mighty heterogeneous force was to come as a surprise to the Turks, just as the evacuation of Suvla surprised them later. The

THE GREAT LANDING 73

East is a huge whispering gallery: how could the knowledge of the careful massing of a vast expedition be smothered? Spies were everywhere, and ever since the bombardment of February 19th the Turks, or, rather, their German leaders, must have foreseen these operations looming. They had had time, and more than time, to provide against them so far as German-Turkish ingenuity allowed. Whether a chance early surprise was universally counted upon, it is impossible to say; the probability is that everything was staked upon the power of our chosen landing parties to seize at the first rush the positions they were ordered to take, and hold, the while the main army was disembarked.

The headland known as De Tott's Battery lies one and three-quarter miles north-east of Seddul-Bahr across an arc formed by Morto Bay. It rises at the highest point almost sheer from the water's edge, but on the land side, going northward, slopes gradually. Still farther North, trending to the southward, a flat, well-wooded patch of country forms the shore edge of the bay, and amid the trees the lofty pillars of an ancient aqueduct stand picturesquely open to the winds.

Captain Davidson, as he tells you in his own little account of the landing, had arranged to put ashore a party of marines and sailors, and this small force had two clear objects—to help the soldiers to disembark and to hold a trench on the left flank whilst the soldiers made their attack, a plan which was momentarily thrown out of gear, for the reason that the *Cornwallis* was held up in getting past the *Agamemnon*, and the soldiers were ashore before our landing party set off.

They left their trawlers when well inside the Straits, noiselessly and with clockwork precision, and embarked in boats towed by the trawlers in lines of six each. When the water shoaled up and the trawlers could go no closer in, the boats were cast off to pull themselves ashore. Two sailors were allotted to each boat, and acted as coxwains and bowmen for the soldier oarsmen, who, cumbered with packs and rifles, lacked freedom for their unaccustomed task. Many of them, of course, had never handled an oar before, but somehow or other they accomplished the feat of grounding the boats a few yards from the land, which, as it then appeared, might have been a desert island.

## THE GREAT LANDING

Into the water up to their middles the soldiers jumped, and a hot rifle fire was opened on them as they dashed ashore and without a moment's hesitation made for the two arranged points of attack, the steep cliff and the slope on the left. It was an unforgettable experience to watch this well-trained battalion working its way methodically and without confusion to the top of the Battery from both sides. Their losses in gaining the crest and making a firm lodgment in the ruins are eloquent of the struggle — fourteen killed and fifty-seven wounded, including Major Margesson and Lieutenant Behrens killed, Captains Johnson and Burkett and Second-Lieutenant Chamberlain wounded.

The *Cornwallis* party arrived just as the South Wales Borderers' right flank was half-way up the cliff, and the thirty-six marines, under Major Frankis, Lieutenant Parker, and Colour-Sergeant Batten in the first boat of the tow, followed the soldiers at once. The sailors, twenty-five of the after-turret's crew, with Gunnery-Lieutenant Minchin, and Petty Officers Jarvis and Clarke, were in the second boat, and as it was their first job to help the soldiers ashore, they ran with hook ropes to the end of the landing to aid those boats which had a longer pull to the beach and were not yet aground.

The marines ascending the hill watched the South Wales Borderers literally fly on ahead, line a wall at the top, place maxim guns in position, run telephone communications down the hill, and station snipers on a line running by a wall at right angles to their position.

Two or three trenches near the combined forces next offered a splendid opportunity for enfilade fire, and one trench surrendered at once; but when a number of the South Wales Borderers went forward to take the Turks prisoners, one of them deliberately opened fire at close range. Immediately a South Wales Borderer put a bayonet through his neck.

The Turks were brought to the rear of our position, and presently the Colonel sent for an interpreter, who bade the spokesman of the prisoners go back to his friends, and tell them if they cared· to surrender they would be well treated and no harm should come to them. This, not unnaturally, the Turk declined to do, saying he would be shot for his pains.

Each time a gun fired from our ships the little group of men drew together.

THE GREAT LANDING 77

" Allah speaks!" they muttered, as though to themselves.

Going down the hill to the boats, a shrapnel from one of the Asiatic batteries burst among the prisoners and killed several. It was this particular gun that Captain Davidson spotted as he ascended the hill. He had its position signalled to the *Cornwallis*, and the ship quickly silenced it.

After the sailors got all boats cleared, the Gunnery-Lieutenant asked Major Going if there was anything else he wanted from the boats, which were exposed to the trench about eighty yards away; and when he said "No," the *Cornwallis* men felt that they had finished their prescribed task, and might be allowed to commence what they afterwards called "a good time."

They all had rifles and ammunition, and keeping carefully under cover, they climbed to the top of the bank and opened fire on the trench, maintaining a position together on the right flank of the company forming the South Wales Borderers' left flank.

After about two minutes of quick firing, a white cloth appeared from the depths of the trench and waved dolorously to and fro. Major

Going did not like the look of it at all—there are white flags and white flags even in Turkey! We fixed bayonets and charged. The sailors, carrying no weight, overtook and passed the soldiers, and were nearly all first into the trench, a very narrow one, five feet deep. Our rush was evidently expected, for of the enemy there was not a sign save a few killed and wounded and two shadowy forms running away up the trench farther to our right.

Suspecting the easy taking of a formidable trench, Major Going ordered everyone out of it, saying he thought it was mined, and as our men jumped out the Turks came to the end of the narrow way holding up their hands. Instantly a dozen sailors prepared to make as many prisoners; but as it was not their business proper, the Gunnery-Lieutenant reluctantly ordered them back, and the soldiers took the enemy in charge.

On then to a small rise ahead, where the sailors were separated from the right and main body by a gully, at the far end of which several enemy snipers lay hidden. During the taking of the rise these snipers accounted for a goodly number of men (among them A. B. Snowden of the *Cornwallis*), and they remained invisible, though a

## THE GREAT LANDING

party under Petty Officer Clarke thoroughly searched the gully and a ruined farm with rifle fire.

And all the time a Battery on the Asiatic side fired on the beach below, never getting a shell inland, fairly plastering the water's edge. The shells did very little damage, as they fell in mud and did not explode, but for all that they helped to isolate the position on the left. Some of the shells fell in shallow water, hit the bottom, and rebounded again, coming out like a trout jumping.

The South Wales Borderers by this time had a firm footing on the Peninsula, and the *Cornwallis* men found time to look about and see how the other near landings were getting on. Sedd-ul-Bahr was a perfect inferno, and the dark silhouette of the *Queen Elizabeth* loomed through a fog of green, black, and yellow smoke as she fired 6-inch broadsides at a terrific rate. Farther round at X Beach troops were seen running in extended order, but it was impossible to tell at that distance whether they were Turkish or British.

The naval party was now recalled. They collected the dead and wounded and took them to the ship. Just as the last boat left the shore, a shell from one of our own ships landed within eight yards of the boat in a bank of mud, and very nearly filled the boat. It had evidently just missed the top of the fort in Sedd-ul-Bahr.

Something must be said of that portion of the *Cornwallis* landing party which was accompanied by Surgeon Galloway and Sick-Berth Steward Brindle. They had an exciting experience, being in the steam pinnace which towed in the galley and two cutters carrying the landing party.

On getting near the beach, the Captain ordered them to stay in the boat and move round to the outer edge of the cliff. After waiting for half an hour in the midst of the storm of shells from the ubiquitous Asiatic battery, Mr. Murphy, boatswain, came alongside in the galley with orders to return to the original position to take up wounded, and the steam pinnace took the galley, into which Surgeon Galloway had stepped, in tow.

When within two hundred yards of the beach, a maxim opened fire from some scrub on the left, and without a word a man in the steam pinnace pitched flat on the deck and two of the galley's crew sank back wounded.

Surgeon Galloway and Brindle landed under

STONE TAKEN FROM FORT 1 AND SET UP ON QUARTER-DECK OF H.M.S. "CORNWALLIS."

1. BOATS FROM "CORNWALLIS" LANDING MARINE BRIGADE, R.N.D., AT KUM KALE, MARCH 4, 1915. WAITING FOR THE ORDER TO GO.

2. ROYAL MARINES ON BOARD H.M.S. "CORNWALLIS" PREPARING FOR THE LANDING FOR THE ATTACK ON DE TOTT'S BATTERY POSITION APRIL 25, 1915.

## THE GREAT LANDING

the cliff and ran round to the left, where they found two wounded S.W.B.'s, one of whom the Surgeon took on his back. The other was able to follow. After stowing the wounded in the steam pinnace, the two indefatigables clambered up the cliff and joined the firing-line, where they dressed the wounded, arriving at a time when the fighting was exceptionally severe.

On board ship the guns were doing all they could to help the attack. Where the landed men were not we fired incessantly, sweeping the woods and level ground to prevent any counter-attack, and trying our best to keep under the rifle fire of the snipers, who were taking cover in the undergrowth fringing the shore, and to put out of action the Asiatic batteries, which from the time the party landed shelled the landing beach and boats. Many stray bullets flew past, but nobody aboard was hit.

Presently signals began to come through from the flagship, urging a move to our second position off the Sedd-ul-Bahr beach, known afterwards as V Beach.

Sedd-ul-Bahr Bay is nothing more than a shallow indentation of the coast at the extreme southern end of the Peninsula, and has as its two boundaries the masonry forts which were reduced in the bombardment and operations of February 19th. To the west lies Sedd-ul-Bahr village, high above the fort of the name, which is perched on the cliff's edge, and eastward the bay ends in another menacing cliff, which drops sheer into the sea and is crowned by Fort Number 1. The distance between the two Forts is about 1,500 yards. The land bordering the shore of the bay is flat in places, going inland for perhaps 200 yards, and then the terrain slopes for another 200 yards to the top of a ridge which dominates the whole shore in a complete semicircle.

Even this bald description will show that no more admirable natural defensive position could have been chosen for attack. Many a time and oft we asked each other, " Why here ?"—a question that can only be answered when the history of the expedition is written and the mind of the Military Staff is laid bare.

*Fiat Lux !*

The landing at De Tott's was well carried out —none better; but that the attack on Sedd-ul-Bahr had been a failure was obvious from where the *Cornwallis* lay. It was not until we arrived at

THE GREAT LANDING 83

V Beach about midday that we realized how matters stood.

The *River Clyde*, afterwards known as "the Dun Cow," by reason of her khaki colour, had gone ashore as arranged with men of the Dublin Fusiliers, Hampshires, and Munsters, Territorial units of the R.A.M.C., and men belonging to the armoured car section R.N.D. on board, towing a steam hopper and alongside lighters which were to form a bridge to the shore from the large ports cut in the collier's sides. When the *River Clyde* struck, the hopper went on under her own steam and momentum, and towed the lighters farther in so as to form the arranged pontoon for the troops to cross. Another body of men in boats were to land from them, and rush the entanglements and trenches, whilst another party on the right took the village of Sedd-ul-Bahr and the fort.

The whole attack was preceded by a heavy bombardment of the Turkish position and trenches by the ships covering Sedd-ul-Bahr, after which the preliminaries of the arranged landing programme were carried into effect.

The Turks allowed the specially cut ports to be opened, and almost as the prepared gangways connected at the bases with the lighters were in position on both sides of the *River Clyde*, the soldiers, in their eagerness to get at the Turks, made a rush ashore. Before many got as far as the lighters (and the few who made the attempt were shot down), almost, indeed, as the men set foot on the gangways, the Turks opened fire with rifles and maxims and pom-poms, and swept our men away wholesale. In heaps our gallants fell on the decks of the lighters, living, dead, and wounded. Some were suffocated and crushed to death by the sheer weight of bodies.

The men in the boats fared no better—they were shot to pieces. Many got into the water, and were drowned by their encumbering accoutrements; others swam to the *River Clyde* or remained in the boats or in the water behind the boats, holding on for hours until they were shot. A certain number from the boats reached the beach, and took cover under a bank which afforded a meagre shelter, and there dug themselves in.

A party that landed at the Camber by the old fort got up to the village of Sedd-ul-Bahr as far as the windmills, and these men, heroes all, gave those of us who were stationed in the tops an example of cool, straightforward fighting.

## THE GREAT LANDING

No trench work was there—it was deer-stalking, with the hunter and the hunted able to deal death. From second to second the life of every soul in that little company depended on quickness of aim, readiness of resource, and skill in taking cover.

Advancing in a series of crawls and short runs, with backs bent double, across an open space between the cliff and a row of houses, our men sheltered as best they could, crouching low against the foundations of anything standing. Opposite them the Turks held a loop-holed wall.

Sometimes one side and sometimes the other bobbed up, and a shot was fired—often not more than ten yards separated the adversaries. And all the while what impressed us breathless onlookers was the adroitness with which our men turned every projecting angle of a house, every fallen stone, every insignificant rise in the road, to account. We who had seen no other land fighting felt that these men of the 29th Division had no superiors among the fighting men of the world. We were not mistaken. Their immortal deeds are engraved for ever on the cliffs they scaled.

The brave little company was driven back, outnumbered; many were cut off, and all the wounded, and on these was wreaked vengeance German-fashion, not Turkish, for the Turks are clean fighters as a rule. This story we had from men who saw the dead later, and swore to the hideous maltreatment.

No amount of shell fire was able to stop the hellish fire of maxims and rifles from the trenches—the Turks were dug in in regular caves, and the ships were too far out to see properly.

It was recognized that any further efforts to land from the *River Clyde* before dark would be disastrous, and the rest of the troops remained in the ship. Had they wished to land it would have been impossible, as the bridge had gone adrift and the lighters broke away in the tide rip. A third lighter, held in reserve, was brought up to fill the gap caused, and this pontoon gave way also, severing the connection with the shore once more. All this time a continuous rifle and maxim fire was being poured on every boat and lighter which approached the shore, and the combination of this and the broken lighters gave opportunities for the heroic acts which won V.C.'s for Commander Unwin, R.N., in

THE GREAT LANDING 87

command of the *River Clyde*; Midshipman Malleson, R.N., of the *Cornwallis.*; Midshipman Drewry, R.N.R.; and A. B. Samson, R.N.R. There were others who did not less readily expose themselves, and numbers of men throughout the ghastly day sacrificed their lives in helping the wounded to shelter.

Commander Unwin bore a charmed life, and jumped repeatedly into the water to salvage lighters and to save drowning soldiers. Midshipman Malleson gained his V.C. for twice swimming with a rope under an appalling fire to one of the lighters which had broken adrift, besides being, as were Midshipmen Weblin and Lloyd (of the *Cornwallis*), in the midst of all the work. Midshipman Drewry the same.

The day was a triumph for the Midshipmen. They were given the opportunity of a lifetime, and no body of men could have risen to the occasion more completely. So said the Australians at Anzac and the soldiers at the other beaches. But all naval ratings did well. As a wounded officer of the Dublin Fusiliers told us, " The naval men were an example to us all." He instanced an A.B. who urged on the soldiers who were being shot down at the oars by saying over and over again, "They won't hurt—they are only small ones."

The men of the *Cornwallis* who underwent the most severe experiences during the landing operations were those who formed the boats' crews for the landing of the soldiers. They joined their boats on the night of the 24th April, and lay in them in tow of trawlers until they went alongside mine-sweepers at daybreak, and filled up with the troops in readiness to be taken in tow by the steamboats of the fleet, six boats forming a tow.

We will follow the third boat in Number 4 tow, and its experiences are typical of what all boats' crews endured.

They steamed towards V Beach, and were slipped within 300 yards of the shore, and up to this point there was no opposition. They were pulling in under their own oars, and the *River Clyde* had just gone aground.

Suddenly a terrific fire was opened on them— the bullets were flying like a storm of hailstones, and the boat's side was riddled. Directly she touched the beach the bowman, Taylor, jumped out with the painter, and he was instantly shot, dying later in Malta Hospital. The few un-

A BRITISH BATTLE-CRUISER INSIDE THE DARDANELLES FIRING AT THE NARROWS FORT.

Two shells from a concealed Turkish battery can be seen striking the water close to the ship

*Central News, Ltd.*

RUINS OF THE FORTRESS OF SEDD-UL-BAHR.

*Central News, Ltd.*

THE GREAT LANDING 89

touched soldiers jumped into the water, and of the thirty-two originally in the boat only three got ashore, a Major, Captain, and Lieutenant being killed or wounded with their men.

By this time there were only two left at the oars—Skitmore, A.B., and Boy Darling, with Leading-Seaman Ford at the tiller. Cragie, A.B., and Boy Runacres were in the bottom of the boat dressing the wounded. Lynn, A.B., had been hit in the leg by a bullet which had first passed through the boat's side, and though he could not move he dressed the wounded who were within his reach. Boy Darling was shot next, and Ford left the tiller and took his oar.

"Cheer up, my son; it will soon be over," he said; and almost immediately a bullet found a billet in his shoulder. He continued to row with one hand, and he and Skitmore between them backed the boat out.

A steamboat came along, which took them to a sweeper, where the wounded were deposited, after which the three unwounded seamen were ordered to collect another load of soldiers, whom they landed under a less heavy fire and with fewer losses. Shortly afterwards the boat was struck by a shell and rendered unseaworthy, whereupon the dauntless three plunged overboard and swam to the *River Clyde*, rejoining the *Cornwallis* in the evening.

The sailing pinnace of the *Cornwallis* followed out the same plan as regards the filling up with troops, and took sixty of the Dublin Fusiliers. The tow to which they were attached was slipped near the *River Clyde*, and they began to pull ashore with their own oars, with five men of the *Cornwallis* to give a professional backing to the unskilled efforts of the loaded-up soldiers.

It was impossible to gather accurate details as to what happened, but the state of the boat when picked up on the following day, full of dead and riddled with holes, showed that the fire under which it came had swept the boat clear of living beings. Every sailor at the oars, with the exception of Ward, A.B., was shot down; and on seeing this, Petty Officer Medhurst, coxwain of the boat, sang out, " Jump out, lads, and pull her in !"

There was only himself and Ward to answer the call, and out the two of them got, one on the port side and the other on the starboard.

Only three soldiers are believed to have got

THE GREAT LANDING 91

ashore—all the others were killed in the boat or in the water as they landed. Two of them saved their lives by remaining alongside Ward in the water under the lee of the gunwale from 7 a.m. to 5 p.m. Medhurst was at first safe, but when the stern of the pinnace swung to the tide, he was exposed to the enemy's fire, and he was not seen again until we recovered his body from the water on the following day.

By the time the *Cornwallis* took up her position off V Beach there was no attacking and no further landing of large numbers of troops, as the impossibility of taking Sedd-ul-Bahr and the ridge was realized. The remainder of the men allotted to V Beach were deflected to W Beach, afterwards called Lancashire Landing.

It was comparatively quiet. There was no movement whatever, except the constant plying to and fro of boats removing the wounded from the *River Clyde*. Numberless dead bodies lay along the beach and in the wash of the waves; the only living men were those who crouched together under a small bank which separated the land from the water's edge. These did not dare to lift their heads above cover, and there we saw them lie all day in the hot sun without food or water except what they may have had on them.

During the day our boats plied backwards and forwards getting off some of the wounded, and we received on board from the *River Clyde* men of the Dublin Fusiliers and the Royal Munster Fusiliers, amongst them being Lieutenant Watts, who was hit ten times when on the lighter, five in the back and five in the arm. He described to us the awful condition under which the landing from the collier was attempted. Nothing could have lived under the converging fire of machine guns and rifles. The Turks had posts, too, marking the range, and barbed wire in the water. Row after row of barbed wire defended the slopes, and of the few men who got ashore many died in trying to cut through it.

During the afternoon we watched the fighting which was going on at W Beach, where earlier in the morning the Lancashire Fusiliers had covered themselves with glory in scaling the heights overlooking the beach. The Essex and Worcester Regiments also landed here, and we witnessed an assault on the trenches guarding the back of Sedd-ul-Bahr which was to render them untenable. Splendid, gallant work—we could see

THE GREAT LANDING 93

the attack on a redoubt and on the wire by Fort I on the top of the ridge. By night they had taken the redoubt, and were digging in.

From 6 p.m. to midnight there was a slight lull, and the men remaining unwounded in the *River Clyde* were got ashore and into the fort or under cover on the foreshore. Stores and ammunition were landed, a few guns also—a mountain battery and a couple of R.H.A. guns.

We had an unusual experience for a battleship in the coming on board of several batches of wounded soldiers—in some cases because they were transported from the shore in our own boats, and were naturally brought on board us as being the nearest available spot; in another case, as it was the middle of the night, it was thought best for their own comfort to take them on board instead of sending them straight to a hospital ship; and in the case of one cutter full of wounded in a piteous state, they had been taken to several hospital ships which were already crammed, and were finally brought to the *Cornwallis*.

We were fortunate in that Captain Le Mesurier, R.N., had, while at Chatham, procured twelve bedsteads which were salvaged from the *Maine*, a hospital ship wrecked before the war. His fore-cabin had been arranged so that the iron bed-posts could be fitted there at half an hour's notice, and before the 25th April, Captain Davidson had ordered the beds to be put up, with the result that we had ready to hand a sick ward with twelve properly equipped hospital beds in it. Nothing could have been more convenient and comfortable. Of each batch of wounded, the worst cases were sorted out and put in these beds; the rest were given mattresses, pillows, and blankets placed in the lobby and on the deck. One night there were so many wounded men that gun-room settees and boats' cushions had to be requisitioned to supply beds for all.

When brought alongside, those who could climbed up the gangway, whilst the stretcher cases were brought up by the quarter-deck davit. It was found that the most convenient form of sling was the strait-waistcoat one, in which the whole body was wrapped round by covered wicker-work and slung on deck in an immovable position.

After having come on board, the wounded either walked or were carried down to the long passages which run both sides fore and aft of the stokers' bathroom. This latter was fitted up as an opera-

THE GREAT LANDING 95

ting theatre, and here, whenever we went into action, the surgeons and sick-berth stewards had everything ready. The place was well under the water-line; there was a good supply of water available, and a high temperature both in it and the passages.

It was most noticeable how quickly the wounded recovered from the effects of shock in the great warmth below decks; it seemed to counteract the collapse, which was normally expected, and the improvement in their condition in a few hours was extremely marked. When they came on board one could not have met a more dirt-covered, tired, weary, and unhappy crowd; but in a short time the appearance and spirit of most of the wounded underwent a wonderful change. These remarks are not the result of the observation of amateurs, but of the medical officers in charge.

Apart from the regular staff, who worked night and day, attendance on the wounded was done by volunteers. On getting below, while waiting for his turn for dressing, each man was given a hot drink, either Bovril, soup, tea or cocoa, prepared in the Ward-room galley. The Ward-room steward and his staff were never too busy or too tired, whatever the time of day or night, to supply and distribute hot drinks and food.

When a wounded man had been dressed and washed, he was taken up to the Captain's cabin or the lobby, and either put in a cot or else given a bed on the deck, according to his state. It was here that the bandmen were more than useful. Under the supervision of their bandmaster, Weedon, they proved excellent sick orderlies, quiet, willing, and attentive. During the night two were always on watch.

The principal medical officer made himself responsible from the sick-bay for the feeding of all who required special food; while Sergeant-Major Batten took in hand the feeding of those who, slightly wounded, were able to eat ships' food.

## CHAPTER VI

### SIDELIGHTS

"This weaves itself perforce into our business."
*King Lear.*

THE tremendous episode of the Great Landing blazes at you from so many facets, is so crowded in every one of its glowing hours with heroic deeds, pathetic incidents, and unflinching purpose, that it is necessary to hold all records of it at a long arm's length to grasp even one aspect of the majestic drama. For this reason we would like, inartistic though it may be from a literary point of view, to include in our account of the work undertaken by the *Cornwallis* at the Dardanelles the personal narratives of some few of the ship's company, and a summary by our Captain of the landing at De Tott's Battery.

The incidents of the Midshipmen's logs, moving as they are, are not depressing. They keep us so close to the spirit of the Old Navy and its traditions that we realize those compensations which, hidden though they may be in a welter of blood and tears, are never absent. And the beauty of the courage displayed shines too steadily throughout for any blows of fortune to repel us.

ACCOUNT BY CAPTAIN A. P. DAVIDSON, R.N.

*Landing of South Wales Borderers at De Tott's Battery to secure the Right Flank of the Army of Invasion of Gallipoli Peninsula.*

The *Cornwallis* was detailed to take about eight hundred men of the South Wales Borderers, Colonel (now Brigadier-General) Casson in command. The general idea of the whole landing was to disembark at several points simultaneously, after half an hour's bombardment. Three ships were detailed as attendant ships, a phrase never explained, but presumably meant that the ships in question—*Euryalus* (Flag), *Cornwallis*, and *Implacable*—remained off the disembarking positions to look after the boats' crews and beach parties, and to support the landing as required.

The *Cornwallis*, however, had an entirely different problem to the *Euryalus* and *Implacable*.

They went straight to their position of disembarkation, and remained there. The *Cornwallis* had to go two and a half miles up the Straits, and after landing the Borderers, and giving necessary support, return to an anchorage laid down to the south-west of Sedd-ul-Bahr.

The problem was further complicated for the reason that, instead of there being a beach party and steamboats to assist in landing the troops on this exposed right flank, none were allowed. The trawlers, four in number, each with six transport boats in tow, were to run ashore as best they could; and the battalion had, by their order, to pull ashore, not only in heavy marching gear, but with boats laden with ammunition, water, and provisions.

This was beyond the powers of any but highly trained men in pulling against a strong tide, and appeared, on the face of it, certain disaster, as the only chance of success lay in speed, and not giving the enemy an easy target. For it was known by air reconnaissances that not only did trenches overlook the beach, but there was a 4-gun battery overlooking it as well, about half a mile inland; and also there were the Asiatic batteries to consider.

So, though tentative arrangements were drawn up between Colonel Casson and myself to insure the South Wales Borderers getting maximum support, it was not until a signal was received at 9 p.m., April 24th, from Rear-Admiral Wemyss, that the *Cornwallis* was to support the Borderers on landing, that the plans were finally and definitely settled. They were as follows:

I made myself responsible for landing as much water, ammunition, and stores as two cutters could take; a beach party from the ship was told off to unload these on arrival, also kits belonging to the Borderers, as it was considered that by their flying light (except for ammunition and water) casualties would be reduced to a minimum, and from having often examined De Tott's Battery, I was of opinion that it could be scaled. This was the key of the position and the right flank.

Colonel Casson determined to take this position as soon as he landed with a company under Major Margesson. (This gallant officer was killed after taking the height.) The rôle of the small Naval Brigade was to protect the left flank of the Borderers and to act as beach party. The *Cornwallis* was to give a thorough searching fire to the whole area as she approached, and then to anchor so as to synchronize landing her men at the same time as the Borderers, and to carry on firing as requisite while the landing was proceeding.

Stress had been laid by me to avoid landing on the beach proper, but as near the point as possible, to avoid fire from trenches.

Events went as jointly planned, but owing to French mine-sweepers and the *Agamemnon* getting in the way, the *Cornwallis* had to reduce speed inside the Straits, and the trawlers, which had embarked the Borderers at 4.45 a.m. on the 25th, crept ahead, and grounded as ordered about the same time as the *Cornwallis* anchored, about 7.30 a.m. The steam-pinnace, with two cutters and galley in tow, Colonel Casson and the Adjutant in galley, landed its Naval Brigade shortly after the boats from trawlers had disembarked their freight. However, our men joined up with the Borderers in time to storm the trenches nearest the beach, and swept on with the Borderers, taking a second trench.

Shortly after the party had landed, the Asiatic batteries became active, and sent a great many shells into the boats that were being cleared by a small party from the Borderers, and into the supports who were waiting for orders to go ahead and taking cover on the wrong side of a ridge, as they naturally thought they were being shelled by guns on Gallipoli.

At this point, thanks to Chief Yeoman Chatwin, who signalled to the ship to open fire at Asiatic batteries (which was promptly carried out), many casualties were averted, and the Captain of the company was good enough to listen to my directions to get over the ridge. Mr. Murphy (bo'sun), who had been working as beach party here, did splendid work by going amongst the Borderers' beach party and getting them to take cover in the right place.

By 10 a.m. the Asiatic batteries had been temporarily silenced. Repeated recalls had been made for the ship to go to her station off V Beach, and as by that time the Borderers evidently commanded the position, and there was only desultory firing and sniping going on, it became an imperative duty for me to withdraw the Naval Brigade and to get off the wounded, about fifty in number.

Gradually the seamen withdrew, covered by the marines, advantage being taken of a lull in the firing from the Asiatic batteries to get everybody embarked. The casualties were very slight considering that a whole Turkish battalion (as known by captured Turkish orders) were detailed to defend Morto Bay.

It will always be a matter of regret to me, in a limited sense, that I was unable to be present and see for myself the conduct of our little Naval Brigade as it disappeared over the ridge with the Borderers. I had no option, not only because of the heavy shelling of the beach by the Asiatic batteries, which had to be silenced, but it was my duty to keep in touch with the ship in case of any further developments, and also I had arranged with Colonel Casson that I would act as beachmaster. However, it was afterwards reported to me by Major Frankis and Lieutenant Minchin that our men behaved in accordance with the best traditions of the Navy; that they assisted in the capture of two Turkish trenches, showed dash and energy, and sustained a loss of two killed and four wounded.

The main point was that the South Wales Borderers took and held the right flank, unsupported, for forty-eight hours. It was a very great relief to the General in command that his right flank was secure, especially in view of the failure of the centre, at V Beach, to make good a landing; and though it will always be a matter of judgment whether the order to support the Borderers was not carried out in too wide a sense, the alternative of a half-hearted support —viz., to let the Borderers run their own show without assistance from the *Cornwallis* in boats and men—would have been, in my opinion, absolutely fatal. And it was the fortune of war that it so happened, on account of the failure at V Beach, the *Cornwallis* was recalled and unavoidable delay took place, which, quite rightly from the naval point of view, was considered inexcusable. No artillery support could have adequately secured this landing at V Beach, and so, though no naval recognition was given to the *Cornwallis* for making good the landing of the Borderers, the fact remains that those on the spot knew, and the responsible Generals knew, that without our efforts the landing at De Tott's Battery Beach would, in all probability, have failed, just as much as the one at V Beach failed; and if the Turks had reinforced and got the high ground at De Tott's Battery, that would have been as difficult to take as Krithia.

## SIDELIGHTS

It is of interest to note that it was because Colonel Casson represented to me that the orders for his landing by his own resources in transport boats meant, in all probability, the absolute annihilation of his battalion before getting ashore, added to the fact that General Hunter-Weston personally informed me that he was entrusting one of his best battalions to the *Cornwallis* to land, and that he placed the greatest importance in securing the right flank, I cast about for a means to avoid any mishap or failure both for the sake of the battalion and for the reputation of the *Cornwallis*, though I was unable to get any steamboats or beach party from official sources.

### BEACH PARTIES' EXPERIENCES. MIDSHIPMAN LLOYD'S STORY.

The transport's life-boat in which I was belonged to the third tow. We were twenty-eight in all on board: some beach parties, some soldiers, and the crew.

We followed the usual routine of boats, being towed in by a picket-boat, cast off, and pulling ourselves to the shore. After leaving the picket-boat, we had got half-way to the shore, when we met Forbes in his boat, who shouted to us to go to the starboard side of the hopper. Before we got there, all the men pulling at the oars were either killed or wounded. Leach, A.B. (*Cornwallis*), though wounded, was the only one still pulling.

(Leach was the " funny man " of the ship, full of real wit and always cheerful. None of us who ever saw him come up to the bridge, looking like a rat-catcher, with woolly headgear and an old plain-clothes coat, will forget the scene. He was wonderful, too, in hospital at Malta, and kept everyone alive; the doctor in charge gave him a bottle of porter a day because he was such a cheery fellow and kept the others merry.)

When we came within fifteen yards of the hopper, an R.N.D. officer shouted to us to jump out of the boat and swim for it. Weblin and I both jumped out and tried to swim to the hopper, but we found our packs too heavy, and returned to our boat. We hung on to the life-lines for a few minutes, as we could not get into her, she was so high out of the water. However, at last Weblin managed to push me over the gunwale; I then pulled him on board, but with the loss of his pack.

While hanging on the lines I got hit, a bullet running under my vest and across my shoulders, just taking some flesh off my shoulder-blade. Also my cap was knocked off.

All this time a very heavy fire was being kept up. Bullets were flying everywhere, some coming on one side and some the other. The boat was riddled, full of bullet holes, and half full of water.

We knew it was hopeless to stay where we were, so we sat at the bottom of the boat in the water, and rowed towards the hopper, pulling with our arms above our heads. We got there all right, jumped out, and secured our boat. Here I got another bullet across the back of the hand.

By this time we were rather exhausted, so sat down under what we thought was cover. But we soon found we were being sniped, so I moved round the corner.

Here I saw Lieutenant Morse, R.N. He called to me to lend him a hand in securing a lighter. So we hauled the lighter astern, giving the stern a kick out so as to meet the other lighters. We both jumped into the lighter; but as she was moving, Morse said: "Have you secured the hawser?" My reply was: "No, sir, I thought you had." So again I jumped out on to the hopper, before the lighter swung out, and secured the hawser round a bollard. Just in time, as I got another bullet through my lung. I spun round and fell down, managing to get more or less under cover. I lay where I was till about 11 a.m., when, coming under machine gun fire, I crawled round to the rear of the hopper.

At this time I saw twenty soldiers making a rush across the hopper from a lighter. The Turks turned a machine gun on to them and killed the lot. Unfortunately for me, I, too, came under this fire. The only bit of me that was exposed was my ankle, which caught another bullet.

I was rescued by a seaman from the *Hussar*—Samson, A.B., R.N.R. (Who later got a V.C. for his work during the landing.) He came out of the engine-room and carried me below. Here I stayed till 10 p.m., knowing very little of what was going on, only hearing from time to time the sounds of the rushing feet of men who made attempts to get ashore.

When I was brought on deck, it was a very bright moonlight night. It felt as if the Turk could not fail to see every movement which was on foot. It was very quiet, no firing, and the troops were getting ashore as fast as they could. I was put into a boat, and was towed, with many others, to a trawler which was close by. We did not get under way till past 11 o'clock, when a terrific rifle and machine gun fire broke out. There had been nothing in comparison with it the whole day. We were, fortunately, under the lee of the *River Clyde*.

This was the general counter-attack which was being made by the Turks all along the line. We heard the yells and shouts away on W Beach. Every man on V Beach was under arms waiting for the attack; and later on the searchlights from the ships began to play, the ships opening fire by their light.

After a short time we got under way, and steamed about till daylight, when we were put on board a makeshift hospital ship. But she was soon full of wounded, and the medical staff was inadequate to cope with the work.

Three days later we were transferred to a proper hospital ship, the *Sicilia*, and arrived safely in Malta.

## BOATS' CREWS' EXPERIENCES. BY MIDSHIPMAN FORBES.

On the evening of the 24th April all boats were provisioned and prepared for the morrow's work.

I was first boat astern of the first picket-boat. Next to me was Midshipman Monier-Williams, in the first cutter. Midshipmen Lloyd, Hardiman, and Weblin were beach party, and went to a fleet-sweeper. Midshipmen Edwards, Last, and Voelcker were running steamboats.

Before dawn on April 25th we were off Helles, and I got into my boat, my crew consisting of Leading-Seaman Baldwin, who was coxswain, Smith, Grosse, Harper, Foam, and Sawyer.

We were towed to the fleet-sweeper *Clacton*, where I got a cup of tea whilst the boats were filling with troops. In about half an hour's time we were being towed by Midshipman Last's picket-boat in charge of Commander Diggle.

As we got in fairly close, we could see the first tows going in to W Beach. A shell from the Asiatic batteries fell just ahead of us, and another from the same quarter behind. In front of us more shells, though only small, were raining down. We passed astern of the *River Clyde*, and being the right flank tow, went in on her starboard side.

About fifty or a hundred yards from the shore the steamboats slowed down, the pulling boats were slipped, and the orders "Oars down!"

"Give way together!" were given, and we were pulling like mad for the beach.

Whiz! A shrapnel burst overhead; everybody ducked. Next second I looked round. Nobody was touched. But going in yet closer we were peppered with the stuff, and a lot of balls fell into the boat.

We were soon alongside the Camber, which was directly under the wall of the fort, and all the soldiers, who were Munsters, jumped ashore and took cover under a wall with no casualties. My boat was the first to beach, likewise the first to get away, and as we went out we received a few more words of cheer in the form of shrapnel.

When we were all in tow once more, we proceeded to another sweeper, and filled up with Royal Naval Division men, and went in a second time—on the port side of the *River Clyde* this journey, and we were slipped when we arrived in line with her stern. As soon as we got fairly close to the shore, we received a warm reception from six maxims or more and four pom-poms, while snipers and troops in the trenches fired incessantly. One of my bowmen had the top of his head shot off, and the other was wounded in both feet. The other four sailors pulled the boat on to the beach, and the instant she touched the soldiers jumped ashore. Many were killed and wounded in doing so, and we had to leave the latter, unfortunately, as there was no time to be lost if the boat was to be got off safely. I made the men sit in the bottom of the boat on stretchers and back for all they were worth, whilst I sat on the bottom of the boat in the stern-sheets and steered. Several bullets passed over my body, and one grazed my right arm. Of the seamen left, one was now hit in the thigh, and another in the arm, so the coxswain took an oar. At last, after what seemed an eternity, we began to glide off the beach, and Harper, who was hit in the arm, now took an oar again, and helped matters greatly; and after being nearly run down by a life-boat, we backed out to where the picket-boat was. Commander Diggle shouted to me to make fast to the stern of the picket-boat, and had I done this the cutter would certainly have been sunk, as shots from a maxim were continually playing just astern of her; so I stayed where I was, out of the line of fire, and the other boats as they got off made fast astern of us. Commander Diggle now got wounded in the knee, and the picket-boat came out and picked us up, towing us straight to the *Aragon*, a hospital carrier.

I took a comprehensive look round. There were two or three soldiers in the boat, one nearly dead and the others wounded, and with one was a little brown dog, who sat beside his master. Three of my boat's crew were wounded badly and a fourth slightly. Grosse was the most severely injured, and he only lived an hour after being hit. Smith was shot in both legs, and I bandaged him up, and did the same for Sawyer, after which I turned my attention to the soldiers. The boat was in a sad state, being about eighteen inches deep in blood and water, with eight bullet holes in her bows and the same number aft. When we at last got to the *Aragon*, I hunted all over the ship for a doctor, but could not find one for three-quarters of an hour, and it was two hours before my wounded were all in-board.

Midshipman Monier-Williams was astern of me in his boat. He had been hit in both thighs, and was severely wounded. That night they gave him up as hopeless, but he pulled through, and went to Malta Hospital later.

I now found the picket-boat ready to tow us back, and we headed for W Beach, as we had been the last tow of boats permitted to go into V Beach. On the way we baled out the boat, and had lunch off chocolate and sardines.

At about 2.30 p.m. we got alongside a trooper, and loaded up with K.O.S.B.'s and Engineers; and as I had only two men to pull the boat and Harper, who still carried on in spite of his wounded arm, I asked for more, and was refused. Some of the soldiers took oars, and we pulled for the beach after the picket-boat slipped us. Things were quite quiet now. The Lancashires had taken the hill and were over the top.

### A Few Words from Engineer-Commander Crichton.

Beyond our steamboats' crews, no call had been made on the Engine-room Department to take active part in the landing operations; all were eager to go, but our duty was clearly on board until occasion should arise for our assistance and services on shore.

About 9 p.m. on the evening of the 26th, we received a signal to send a coppersmith to repair damaged pipe in the *River Clyde*, and such a definite request precluded sending any engineer officer. By 9.30 C. E. R. A. Stevens and Stoker

SIDELIGHTS 115

Gordon were on the way with clips, patches, wire, blanks, etc., to carry out the necessary work, *in situ*, if possible, or remove and blank pipe for repair on board. Instructions were also given to find out if we could be of any further assistance, and in our hearts we hoped there might be some occasion for sending engineer officers. Stevens returned on board at 11 p.m., bringing damaged pipe. It had been shot away, disabling the forward winches. We took the work in hand at once, cutting out the defective parts and flanging the ends, and, by annealing and altering the bend slightly, were able to work it in to "set," and replaced all as good as new in the early morning, to the satisfaction of everyone concerned.

News had also been brought of difficulties experienced with pumps and water delivery on shore. I decided that an engineer officer should go over and sketch the system, and see what arrangements could be made and if any distilling plant had been fitted.

A message had also been received from Commander Unwin asking for assistance in filling and placing water-tanks on V Beach. A strong party was made up, consisting of Engineer-Lieutenant-Commander Cooke, Artificer-Engineer Abbie,

Chief E. R. A. Stevens, E. R. A.'s Cameron and Moss, Leading-Stoker Barnes, Stokers Gordon and Craig, and the watch-keepers were employed in their spare time over-hauling and refitting such cocks as we could muster on board. Fortunately, we found a good many, and were able to send enough to complete one section of tanks with the party in the morning.

Other work was also in progress—fitting an eighty-ton water-tank with a pump, a real contrivance, but a good sound job, in which all took great pride; we thought how her arrival would refresh and cheer our comrades on V Beach, and hustled on the work. With the ship's name painted in letters a foot long, with eighty tons of the best distilled water in her hold and her pump heaving beautifully, she was ready. However, being the first completed, she was appropriated to W Beach, and we never saw her again.

In the afternoon, Engineer-Lieutenant-Commander Cooke and Mr. Abbie returned to the ship, bringing sketches and details of pumps, pipes, etc., and we decided to carry out some alterations which would enable a small pump in the engine-room to be used for boiler feed and the large one kept for beach and upper deck supply.

The distilling capabilities had also been inquired into, and it was found the *River Clyde* possessed a small evaporator, a crude arrangement that had been fitted to the tank in the engine-room while at Mudros, but entirely inadequate for its purpose, and we were all for utilizing the main condenser for distilling.

As the ship's fittings were more or less ready, I went over later in the afternoon to see what work was entailed in fitting connections and giving them a trial, and having seen our party all started on work in hand, I went to consult with Commander Unwin and Captain Storey regarding water and the need for husbanding the supply already in *River Clyde*. A good workable scheme was drawn up whereby only drinking water was taken from tanks, and horses watered at village well, sentries being placed and notices and directions being chalked up, and the wells likewise marked.

V Beach was a lively spot, especially towards sunset, when the light seemed to favour the Turkish gunners, and several rounds of small shell plopped about in the water and mud, freely sprinkling them all around. Our naval party carried on through all with a delightful nonchalance, and after a short time it eased down. I did not see a shell burst: they simply slithered and disappeared in the mud; but I heard later that some curio-hunters, digging one out, pressed the button all right with dire results.

All our men now busy and work detailed and arrangements made, I and my messenger went up to the trenches to see what could be seen. I was much struck by the thoroughness of the defences. The wire entanglements were well put up, and secured to iron railings, which had evidently formed some garden fencing of the neighbouring town.

The Turkish trenches were fairly deep, but very narrow, and the dug-outs strongly constructed, and the roofs reinforced by rails and sleepers.

Many winter comforts, such as helmets and mittens, were scattered in all directions, clearly showing that there had been no lack of clothing; and, indeed, all the Turks I saw were well dressed and very clean, not at all unlike our own weather-beaten troops. It was difficult to tell them apart at any distance.

The Turks seemed to have been living on beans and tomatoes, huge tins of which were scattered here and there. I did not have much time to look around, my chief object being to get any little curio for my men who were busy below, to whom, as an incentive to "smack it about," I promised to fetch something. We were fortunate enough to get a little memento for each.

The setting sun now warned us to return, and leaving our soldier friends in the trenches, we sped down the hill and through the village to the beach. There I found such good progress had been made that only one cock remained to be tightened up, and Stevens had all his sets ready and the pipes in position. There was little else to do but check over the details, collect our gear, and get a boat off, which we did, our movements being livened by the "evening hate." But where was our Padre? I had been told to keep a lookout for him, so hunted the beach high and low, and eventually found Lieutenant Morse, who told me our Padre and a military chaplain had just gone off in another boat.

All my men collected, and my mind at rest regarding their Reverences, we steamed off to the ship, arriving on board about 8.30, after quite an interesting afternoon.

Once on board, we carried on preparing pipes, and in the afternoon of the 28th had all connections made and conveyed into trial of the ship's distilling plant. The output was totally inadequate. Very little steam could be dealt with by the crude distiller already fitted, and any attempt to increase the output boiled the water in the tank. I then decided to carry out our original intention, and Engineer-Lieutenant Newhouse was landed to sketch the simplest method to connect the main condenser direct if possible, but failing a ready connection, we intended to pass steam through engines. This latter plan was adopted by removing slide-valves, and ballast donkey was refitted and used for circulating, and we were able to run a trial of the new arrangement. The work was carried on with, and on the 5th May we were running trials and boiling out the system with the free use of lime, so that by the 6th our samples were pronounced by Dr. Irvine free from all impurity, and good drinking water was being made at the rate of three tons per hour, which we considered very satisfactory. Our only concern was that inlet might become choked if *River Clyde* settled; but to guard against this a wooden coffer dam was designed to fit the ship's side, and so carry suction to within a foot of the surface. But whether this was done I know not, as the

SIDELIGHTS 121

*Cornwallis* was ordered to take up another position outside, and could not, to our great regret, keep in touch with the contrivance, which, I afterwards heard, had fallen into disuse.

AN IMPRESSION. BY T. STEVENS, E.R.A.
(Now Artificer-Engineer.)

Our troops having effected a landing at Sedd-ul-Bahr, we received a signal the next day from the *River Clyde*, " Steam-pipe burst; send assistance," and I was despatched at once with Gordon (leading stoker) to the scene of trouble to inspect, report, and, if possible, repair the damage.

As we arrived with our tools and material, the *River Clyde* was having a rough time from the Turkish shells on the Asiatic coast. They were falling thick and fast, the ship was getting badly battered, and daylight could be seen through her in many places.

Steam was heard escaping from the interior, and on examination I found that quite a number of pipes had suffered; and we got to work forthwith, and did the best we could under limited circumstances.

A large shell suddenly passed down through the deck above, cutting a huge hole in the waste-pipe, and, taking with it eighteen inches of the auxiliary steam-pipe, went through the fore and aft bulkhead, finally ending its career in a heap of coal-dust, where our little forge was standing. Fortunately, it did not explode. The following day three more shells passed clean through the ship above the water-line, taking one man's head off and wounding four others.

The repairs and alterations carried out lasted a week, and during that time the fighting never ceased: fast and furious it raged ashore. One shell falling at Sedd-ul-Bahr killed five men, ten horses, and blew up an ammunition waggon.

Many is the yarn, pathetic and humorous, we heard of an evening round our little forge among the coal-dust and lighted candles in the *River Clyde*. The reliefs would straggle down from the trenches, which at this time were not far away, and, coming up the gangway on board, would see the cheery fire and gather round in the dull light—brave men all, who, only a short while ago, were engaged in a life-and-death struggle with the enemy. Tired, hungry, and often wounded, they would find tins of all shapes and sizes, fill them with water, and proceed to cook their evening meal of tinned beef and biscuits boiled together, which they called a "potmess." Outside the ship could be heard the incessant crack! crack! of the rifles, the loud booming of the artillery, and the ships' guns.

Presently, in the midst of an exciting yarn, a fellow, looking round with an inquiring glance, cried out:

"Hello, Jim! Have you seen anything of Jock?"

"No; didn't he come along with you?"

"I haven't seen him since we made that last rush and took that trench. Poor devil! He must have gone under. Is this all there is of us?"

"Yes; there's only the corporal, me, you, and Ginger left out of our lot. Half a mo! What's that long snaky bloke's name—him as outed that Turk with the butt end of his rifle? Lord! wasn't it a whack, and didn't he squeal! He's a gone coon, I bet. You remember when our orficer and Stripey got shot? That's where Jock dipped. Poor old Jock! They do say as how Scotsmen are mingy, but Jock always shared out his fags, and you know how short we were of them, don't you?"

A weary Frenchman arrived on the scene, covered in dirt, with a tin in his hand.

"What cheer, Froggy! Had a rough time of it, matey?"

The Frenchman stood, with an infinite tiredness in his pose, holding up his tin, which had liquid in it, and asking for *sucre*.

"What does he want, Ginger? Tea, I suppose. Here yah, mate; have a wet of this."

"Sucre!" said the Frenchman slowly—"sucre!"

"Garn! it's bread he wants—no, he don't. Hanged if I know how to suit him."

I gave him some of my sugar, and the weary face smiled gravely.

"Merci, monsieur, merci."

The men laughed all together.

"Why, of course it was sugar he wanted all the time. Didn't we say so?"

He placed the sugar in the tin with his wine, warmed it on the fire, and, turning round, drank to our success.

By that time many of the soldiers had fallen asleep on the coals. I wondered what they would dream about—home or battles.

## CHAPTER VII

OF THE DEAD—AND OF THE LIVING

THE night following the historic attack has ascendancy over other dates at this period in the minds of all the ship's company, just as the 25th April will ever make the strongest appeal to our patriotic memory.

There was one continuous roar of rifle fire rolling and reverberating up and down all the scales of sound. From midnight to dawn, hour after hour the hideous din rioted without ceasing through the darkness, the maxims now and again dominating with their querulous hammer.

The Turks were furiously attacking all the positions occupied by us during the hard-won day. It was the same story all along the line. Y Beach, on which the K.O.S.B.'s and a battalion of marines had landed, was desperately hard pressed, and X Beach was barely saved after the fiercest fighting and by the assistance given by the *Implacable*. For some reason the military had requested the ships not to use searchlights, and it was only when our troops ashore asked for naval help that the *Implacable* switched on her lights. Captain Lockyer ran his ship as close in shore as possible, and at a range of a few hundred yards fired salvoes at the Turks, thus saving the situation.

There was more than a chance that the Turks would drive our men on V Beach into the sea and rush the *River Clyde*. Every available man, sailor and soldier, was turned out of her and ordered to line the bank.

As dawn broke the inferno of sound died away. Our men above Sedd-ul-Bahr had lost the redoubt, but still held on.

Sedd-ul-Bahr was always secretive-looking and mysterious with its invincibly gloomy grey fortress " half as old as time," and the sea in sheeted silver at its feet; but this morning, as the sun vanquished the haze and heat and light filled the place, the cinnamon-coloured landscape took on an appearance we never saw again.

It knew nothing then, after all! Nothing of that wild night of desperate effort, nothing of the death-grip of the day before, of the uncovered graves of the resting dead.

The sudden rattle of maxims buried in the hillside gave the answer. With a kind of gasp one awoke as from a dream: Sedd-ul-Bahr was but cogitating in between moments of fitting together the pieces of a difficult puzzle.

And presently our men in the *River Clyde* commenced the attack which ended in the capture of the whole semicircle of ridge and forts commanding the beach. For an hour previously the *Albion* and ourselves swept the slopes with a heavy fire. The traverse trenches were spotted; we could see the Turks moving in them, and until our men got to the top of the ridge, when we could fire no more for fear of hitting them, we and the *Albion* continued to pour a hail of shell on the enemy.

The first we saw of the attack was a little company of men making a dash up the centre from the ledge encircling the beach, and then taking cover. Such a thin line, so very few; but more and more men joined up, and the line stretched out and grew on the slope below the old fort. Everywhere was a maze of barbed-wire entanglements, and we were told afterwards by the Lieutenant in command, of a corporal of magnificent physique who attacked the carefully laid wires with his naked hands and wrenched support after support from the ground under the hottest fire. This hero was killed as they gained the top.

The barbed wire used by the Turks in Gallipoli, German no doubt, was of a kind we had not seen before. Its centre wire was enormously thick, and at the closest intervals strong sharp barbs of unusual strength were well twisted on to the main strand. The formidable spikes were capable of dealing serious wounds, and as compared with the barbed wire used at home it was as rope to cotton.

For ten, twenty, thirty yards at a time we watched groups of men rush forward and throw themselves under the little cover they could find. A small ravine on the left centre, though a network of wire, was a helpful shelter, and gradually the bottom of the last ridge was reached and the soldiers collected together for the final rush. From all sides they came. We could see the bayonets flash in the sun, and it made every ounce of blood in us boil with excitement as the men prepared to assault. It is impossible to describe the intensity of those moments, the waiting as the men strengthened their line and

STORES ON V BEACH AND "RIVER CLYDE."

1. EXTERIOR OF SEDD-UL-BAHR FORT.
2. INTERIOR OF SEDD-UL-BAHR FORT AS SEEN ON APRIL 26, 1915.

OF THE DEAD—AND THE LIVING 129

finally charged and carried the trenches and the old fort.

Surely the spirits of the ancient heroes of Greece and Troy, Hector, Achilles, and Agamemnon, brooding over the classic green plains of Ilium on the Asiatic coast, found these modern Homeric fighters strangely akin.

It was a theoretical attack effected with clockwork precision, and nothing could exceed our admiration for the soldiers who, after enduring about thirty-six hours of hell's fire, undertook this assault unflinchingly. True, the Turks were reduced and their fire much silenced, but the trenches were still held and supposed to be mined. Colonel Doughty-Wylie,* who led the attack, was killed almost in the moment of victory. Thus was Sedd-ul-Bahr taken, a position held (according to an order found upon a dead German officer) by General Liman von Sanders to be impregnable.

On the evening of the 26th, Mr. Murphy, our Bo'sun, made an expedition to Morto Bay, and took provisions and water to our friends the South Wales Borderers, approaching the beach with

* Mrs. Doughty-Wylie, who was in charge of a British hospital attached to the French, was the only woman to visit the Peninsula during the occupation. She was allowed to see her husband's grave at Sedd-ul-Bahr.

muffled oars, as there was constant sniping and the shore was within reach of shell fire from the Turkish trenches.

Over two hundred wounded passed through the ship, and among them were three Turks, one of whom was fighting still in his delirium; for during his first night aboard, when his countrymen were making their great effort to push us into the sea, he flung himself on a wounded Britisher in the next cot and tried to throttle him. The sick-berth steward intervened just in time and pulled the excited assailant away; but the effort was the Turk's last, as in the exertion his wounds opened afresh and he bled to death before anything could be done for him. We buried him at sea next evening, also twelve of our own people, including Lieutenant-Commander Pownall, R.N., who had been Beachmaster at Sedd-ul-Bahr Camber.

All day and all night the landing of men, guns, stores, and ammunition proceeded, and we fired almost continuously on the Asiatic batteries and the Turkish positions on Achi Baba, about five miles inland—the peak of our desire, until one lost count of days and events, and excitements telescoped.

OF THE DEAD—AND THE LIVING 131

The French landed at Sedd-ul-Bahr from Kum Kale on the Asiatic side, which they had taken on the historic Sunday and now evacuated of set purpose, after holding the place long enough to divert the attention of the Turks from the Gallipoli landings. They did a good bit of work after a secure footing in Kum Kale had been obtained— they had landed three thousand to four thousand men—in the contriving of a wire entanglement in front of their position, and a better still in keeping the obstacle a secret from the enemy, who hurled themselves on to it in masses during the night attack, and were shot down by the French in hundreds. The Mendere River bridge was also destroyed, and about five hundred Turkish prisoners taken.

Some of us went ashore in the forenoon of April 27th, and walked through the ruinous village of Sedd-ul-Bahr, picking our way between the dead bodies of Turks and some of our own men, mostly Hampshires. Two comrades lay alongside a wall in front of a barricade, and in their position was the history of their end. Two yards more and they would have gained the shelter of a broken-down doorway.

All about us were pathetic illuminations of

what the fight must have been, distinctive tragedies which pieced themselves together as one looked for the clue; sermons—in stones, too, as a barricade built by our men under the hottest fire declared. It was a monument to bring tears to the eyes—a wall raised across a narrow street by the pushing out of single stones from the precarious refuge of a ruined house. One by one the small pieces of rock, stones, and bricks had been placed in position by the butt-ends of rifles until at last a flimsy cover allowed a man to creep behind it and continue operations. Higher and higher the soldiers had constructed their little fortification, longer and longer until it stretched across the road, a wall as immortal as ever Balbus builded.

In Fort 1 lay the remains of the 9·2 gun which we are convinced the *Cornwallis* knocked out in the bombardment. There it reposed—a gun that was.

More and more, as we wandered about a position which only two days ago had been in the hands of the enemy, we marvelled at the manner of its taking. The whole conduct of the landing was so magnificent in its plucky determination that one almost lost sight of its strategic aspect.

OF THE DEAD—AND THE LIVING 133

Had it one ? Ah, there's the rub! Stronger points of resistance than V Beach do not exist, and the cost of taking it was consequently heavy. The collier appealed to the military mind as a simple means of getting two thousand men ashore quickly, and any opposition, they supposed, would be silenced by the naval gunfire. It sounded so easy.

It is not certain that the military Powers that Were did not place too great reliance on the guns of the fleet, both on this and on other occasions. The naval guns could do much to help, but with the point of aim more often than not invisible, and the necessity of firing from a continuously shifting platform as the ship swung to the wind or tide, it stood to reason that their accuracy and utility could not equal guns in close touch with the troops and with a clear field of operations before them.

Our Chaplain was approached by a Staff officer, who asked about burying some of the dead collected near the beach, and later, when the grave was ready, the Padre, with an army chaplain, attended.

It was a gruesome business, and the stench was awful, as all the bodies had lain in the sun for two days, and some had been in water. In one grave two hundred and four men were buried, and in a smaller, quite close by, five officers.

Shells began to fall, and the burial-party retired to what cover they could find until comparative peace reigned again. The moon was up as the Chaplain quoted from the Prayer-Book he could not see to read, and the "Last Post" rang out to an accompaniment of deep guns booming and the cracking of rifles in the distance.

It had been arranged that V Beach was to be left entirely to the French; and our friends the Borderers, who had been without support since the landing, though they held their own like the gallants they were, moved from the right on to the left flank, handing over De Tott's Battery to the French.

It is impossible to fit words to our remembrance of the speed at which we crossed from anxiety to elation and back again on the Wednesday after the landing. It was a day of initial successes opened by our shelling the village of Krithia and Achi Baba and the slopes short of it with 12-inch. Our troops at this time held a line of trenches from above De Tott's past a reservoir and on to the sea in the north.

Presently the advance on Krithia commenced. The soldiers took the village, but failed to hold it for lack of ammunition, and were driven back in considerable confusion to their original position with severe losses, the Worcesters and the Dublins suffering especially heavily. Early in the afternoon General Hunter-Weston reported to Sir Ian Hamilton that the advance was checked, and that a counter-attack was taking place which could not be withstood owing to shortage of ammunition.

The French, it appeared, had had to fall back, and the Turks at once filled the gap between the Allies and enfiladed the British troops, catching the Worcesters in a hot flank fire. The retirement after this was precipitate, and the end of the day found our men in the same place as in the morning, with severe casualties to their account.

We made two expeditions ashore. Early in the afternoon Dr. Irvine went to Morto Bay to help with the French wounded; there were some four hundred waiting. Three trawlers full were got off, and the doctor did not return on board until 2 a.m. next morning, having been dressing wounded without cessation for the whole of the time. The second trip was an errand of mercy organized by the Chaplain and Lieutenant-Commander Courage, who had heard that the stretcher work of the R.A.M.C. had broken down, and that the wounded were not coming in too well. After obtaining permission from the Captain, they made up a volunteer party to go to the front with stretchers, and the little company landed about seven in the evening.

The road to the troops was difficult to find, and the party, bearing too much to the right, found themselves among the French.

As Courage stood on a bridge studying the lie of the land, a slim figure sped by him, and in the half-light the flying form outlined itself as a Turkish sharpshooter making for some close cover ahead. To call out to a French sentry was the work of a moment, but the Turk had a good start, and another sniper was added to the number already hidden away behind our lines.

A turn to the left through a mysterious, unknown country, which looked in the sombre darkness a savage wilderness of mud and juniper scrub, without a sign of cultivation anywhere, discovered to the seekers three badly wounded men just behind the firing-line. They were taken

GUN KNOCKED OUT BY H.M.S. "CORNWALLIS."

FO'C'SLE OF "CORNWALLIS" DURING A LULL IN THE BOMBARDMENT.

OF THE DEAD—AND THE LIVING 137

up, and Lieutenant-Commander Courage, with Mayo, sick-berth steward, went into the trenches, and brought out a fourth soldier.

How they got back they hardly knew themselves. It was pouring with rain, and there were only two or three men to each stretcher. The mud in places was knee-deep, and the greasy soil squelched under the feet. It was a struggle to go a hundred yards without putting the stretcher down, and in one case it took eight men to lift a stretcher up a bank sleeked with damp clay, which gave no hold at all.

It was two or three miles as the crow flies to the landing-place, and a couple more were added as the party struck this way and that through a tangle of ravines, slippery paths, and rain-swept plateaux, such as one would have supposed no man possessed the secret of. But Mayo went forward readily in the dark, like a man climbing into his own hammock, while from behind, the rest assisted with geographical comments and advice.

They found forty-three wounded men had already come on board—Worcesters, Dublins, Munsters; and later, when their dressing was completed, thirty-five Frenchmen arrived with

Irvine, and we all turned out to find accommodation for the new batch.

There is little doubt that if the Turks had made a determined attack that night our forces hereabouts would have been driven right back. They were dead tired, the regiments were mixed up, and there was very little ammunition. The whole way from the ship to the front line our volunteer party never came across any reserves or reliefs, or supplies of ammunition or provisions.

It was our invariable scheme to open fire on the Asiatic ridge directly they began dropping shells on V Beach and the *River Clyde*; for we looked upon ourselves as the protectors of this position, inasmuch as the reason for our presence was to supply a ready depôt for the trawlers, steamboats, lighters, and provision boats, which were constantly engaged in disembarking troops, horses, guns, and stores.

Though the batteries could range on Sedd-ul-Bahr, they seldom fired at the *Cornwallis*, and thanks to the inferiority of the Turkish or German ammunition, 90 per cent. of the shell from the Asiatic batteries did not burst. The *Agamemnon*, which was hit and lost one man killed and ten wounded, knocked out one of these Asiatic guns, but another was in position immediately.

We had Lawrence, Reuter's representative of the provincial newspapers, living aboard us. Ashmead-Bartlett, who represented the London papers, was in the *London*, appropriately enough. This ship landed the Australian and New Zealand contingents on the 25th at Gapa Tepe. Ashmead-Bartlett dined with us one night, and gave us the first reliable information of the Over-Seas forces and the getting ashore.

There is one thing about him besides the quality of his writing which commended him to us all—he doesn't know the meaning of the word " fear." A great talker—he talked us all dumb—he is the personification of the type of self-assured bounce who would get round the world on a sixpence, and write a book about it afterwards explaining how he did it. It was the famous correspondent's belief that if we offered ten shillings cash to every Turk who surrendered with a rifle and ammunition they would all come in, and for a fiver we should get a maxim. Well, there was something in the idea, whimsical as it sounds. The Turk is essentially a mercenary.

It was Ashmead-Bartlett's privilege to write

an account of the Australian landing which rang through the world. It was an inestimable privilege, for, after all, the thing that lives in history is not the event: it is the written account of it.

The enemy aeroplanes, German piloted, were suddenly galvanized into unwonted activity, and tried to drop bombs on the stationary air balloon ship. These fell three hundred yards from us— no damage to anyone. There was no hitting the cursed gnats. In France they say successful gunners wait for the suggestion of a poise, which follows on the throwing of a bomb, all the chance a skilled airman ever supplies. Enemy aeroplanes with us never did any of this "poising"; they darted away every time, and we had hairbreadth escapes and aerial chases going on most days.

From the shore came to us stories of the losses caused by snipers—a source of annoyance during the early days of the occupation. Somehow that sniper dressed in green leaves and merging into the landscape had an attraction of his own. One could imagine him changing his brown face to green and surrounding it with a halo of leaves greener still, hanging olive-branches round his shoulders, and outing a rabbit from a near-by burrow. And then the hours of eye-strain from peering through cracks in the sand, or backbreaking hours with his ears glued to the ground. The impassioned days of responsibility, too; the feeling: "I am what I am—the man on whom this show depends, its Alpha and Omega, its Nadir and Zenith. In fact, the whole dam thing!"

An emerald-green sniper tucked away in a burrow, with his fourteen days' provisions and cartridge clips full, has the ingenuousness of ingenuity; but there were others with nothing to recommend them, habitual criminals who fixed rifles on tripods overlooking well-used paths and pressed the trigger as anyone passed a certain bearing. Another common trick was to feign death—a successful ruse, for a dead Turk more or less occasioned no suspicion. Rumour told of a body of six who were playing 'possum in this fashion, and unfortunately for them one of them moved as some soldiers went by.

"I'm not sure about this man, sir," said the corporal dubiously.

"Make sure!" replied the officer grimly. "Make sure!"

All kinds of visitors gravitated to the *Cornwallis*.

Now it was a company of fifteen Greeks working on the lighters ashore, who brought with them most unwelcome additions to the ship's company—fleas as big as hens and other entomological specimens. A dirty-looking lot of men, they were caught trying to desert to the Turks.

We were none too well pleased at having to surrender to the flagship two captured Turkish pom-poms which had been brought on board and made serviceable. It was our desire to hand them over to the two battalions which had taken the ridge above Fort 1 where the guns were found.

## CHAPTER VIII

### THE DIN OF ARMS

A VERY heavy attack was made by the Turks all along the line on the night of May 1st, and lasted from 10.30 to 5 o'clock in the morning. The rolling of the rifles sounded like some gigantic hammering machine pulsing in dull beats, and swelled in a continued volume of noise, punctuated by the even reports of a battery or two of the French ·75's, which remind one of a door banging sharply. The naval guns broke heavier, " more manly like," to use the words of one of our petty officers. Shrapnel burst over Sedd-ul-Bahr and De Tott's in showers of fireworks, and in different directions star-shells displayed their brilliant white light and lit up the sky before they fell. Those of us on deck were fairly praying for dawn. A signal had come through at 3 a.m. saying that the French were being driven back. For the rest, we had to wait for the light. Would it never be morning !

Sixty British and French wounded were brought on board, and from them we gathered something of the fight ashore. Our line had been penetrated, but from what we heard it seemed that after the Turks had broken through the line was re-formed and a number of Turks and ten German officers were cut off and taken prisoners. This proved to be approximately correct. A small advance was made in a counter-attack, and the Turks lost heavily. Their dead, it was said, lay in hundreds before our lines.

Directly it was light the ships began shelling to keep down the fire of the enemy, and in this we were successful, as about 7 a.m. it ceased altogether. The net result of the night's work, according to General Hunter-Weston's report, was a gain of five hundred yards for us and one thousand for the French.

A new phase began in connection with the firing of the ships on the Asiatic side, when for the first time adequate aeroplane observation was available, and the results showed the value of such methods as compared with the haphazard ones hitherto used. Where guns can only be knocked out by direct hits on the guns themselves an error of five yards makes all the difference,

TURKISH GUN IN RUINS OF SEDD-UL-BAHR FORT.

SEDD UL BAHR FORT IN DISTANCE. EMPTY SHELL CASES IN FOREGROUND.

THE DIN OF ARMS 145

and such minute errors could not be spotted from the ships, even at the comparatively short range of five thousand yards. The satisfactory consequence was seen in the *Agamemnon* knocking out three 6-inch guns near a red-roofed farm on the Asiatic ridge. The *Prince George* too, though hit herself, was most successful and accounted for a couple of tireless guns.

Very many men died aboard all the ships other than their own companies, and fleet burials were on a wholesale scale those summer days. A funeral trawler collecting from the hospital ships and transports would make the round of the warships in the late afternoon, a Chaplain, an officer as mourner, and a firing party accompanying each freight. After being carefully sewn up in the white sail-cloth we use for the purpose, bodies were collected in one of the 6-inch casemates and lay there for two or three hours, perhaps, waiting their last journey; and in the midst of a series of sights which tended to make one regardless of death there were few more impressive than the bringing forth of the mummy-like forms, each with its name-label fluttering in the wind. Through the batteries aft between groups of men off duty, playing cards maybe, having a little sing-song, or idly smoking, the procession passed, led by a bugler sounding the "Attention." Cards were dropped, the sing-song died away, pipes were laid aside, eclipsed by a Presence in which was drawn together all the far-stretched greatness, all the pride, cruelty, and ambition of man.

Generally a gangway was managed to the waiting trawler, and down this the corpses were carried on stretchers and laid with the others on the foc's'le.

Though the fighting ashore was continuous by day, night attacks were evidently the Turkish idea of how best to overcome us. Monday night, May 3rd, ushered in another determined adventure, which ended, as had all the others, in the Turks being driven back. The assault was hottest on the right, and some progress was made against the French. We engaged the Asiatic batteries until 1 a.m., and often as they replied so often we fired, until at last it was borne in on us that for some part of the time at least the recurring flashes were dummies. They were so clear that one felt instinctively a German-trained Turkish gunner would have concealed his position more carefully. This was practically verified next day, as the Captain discovered that such dummy batteries existed.

## THE DIN OF ARMS

Dawn found the Turks advanced close to the French, and the *Lord Nelson* opened on them with 12-inch shrapnel—probably this was the first occasion it had been used in the Navy. The effects were extraordinary. Numbers of the enemy were destroyed and many left their trenches and surrendered rather than face the deadly spread. Seen through glasses from our ship, the area covered by the bursts of shrapnel was enormous—five hundred yards at least. The *Cornwallis* had shrapnel for her 6-inch guns only, but had we possessed shrapnel for the 12-inch we could have saved hundreds of lives and the attacks on the batteries also would have been more successful. The *Queen Elizabeth* had shrapnel, though we did not see her fire any, and one of her shells, it is said, contains 13,700 bullets!

A heavy fire was kept up through the morning from the Asiatic shore on V Beach and the *River Clyde*, and it was wonderful how little damage had been done on this congested beach during the continuous landing of thousands of men and horses. The officers and men who had lived in the *River Clyde* since the memorable 25th were battle-tuned veterans now—they hardly heard or noticed the shells at all.

Our line had been in much the same position for a week, but guns and men were arriving daily, and at the back of everyone's mind was the cheering thought: "We shall advance before long."

For a day the *Cornwallis* was absent from her post the while she took in ammunition at Mudros, and on our return to the old spot off V Beach the officers living in the *River Clyde* told us they had been under the heaviest fire of the last week from the Asiatic batteries, and they missed the ship's counter fire. We had an unrivalled knowledge of the position of batteries, as from the earliest days our gunnery and observation officers had closely watched and studied the Asiatic shore.

The familiar Germanic efforts at faked signals were now prevalent. "Send all boats at once— French in full retreat!" could not be traced to any Franco-British source. On another occasion a voice calling in the trenches, "This way the Essex," caused the Acting-Colonel to rise up in an attempt to see who had given the order. He was shot dead.

All sorts of minor interludes made up our strenuous days. Aeroplanes visited us and were chased away; our submarines were reported to be active, but results were still unknown; mines

THE DIN OF ARMS 149

adrift were sighted and destroyed; the flanking ships came in for a good deal of fire, and the *Albion* and *Prince George* were slightly damaged.

Soldiers of some of our regiments who were in the Mons retreat, and Frenchmen who were at the Marne, told us that those fights were child's-play to the Peninsula battles. One discounted this, as it might be due to the smallness of the terrain and the concentration of the fighting, but there is no doubt it equalled anything that had occurred during the war. And from our vantage ground of the ship we saw two things clearly: that nothing can be said too laudatory of the valour of our men, sailors and soldiers—no country can produce better; and that nothing absorbs a man more than fighting—the interest is compelling.

The 6th, 7th, and 8th May were all marked by heavy fighting. Two brigades of Australians and New Zealanders came round by sea from Anzac to join the British troops and an Indian brigade joined the firing line. There grew up between the Anzacs and the Indians, possibly from a mutual admiration of each other's fighting qualities, an *entente* which was specially noticeable by those who watched the two forces together.

Preliminary plans involved the taking by the

French of the ridge behind De Tott's Battery, for this ridge was in a position to enfilade Krithia, which could not be held until the vantage ground was in our hands.

In most of the attacks we participated with guns that would bear, directed by signals or else by our own spotting. We could see little of the forward movement—the fighting was more or less out of sight and hearing of the ship, except for the falling shell and the hammering of rifles and maxims.

The French attacked strongly and appeared to advance to the very crest of the ridge, but about 4 o'clock they were driven back. They may have made progress in the evening, as we were told they would, but no news came through of this. The results that night seemed disappointing.

Krithia was not taken.

The *Agamemnon* did her best to make up for our frustrated hopes, and knocked out more guns on the Asiatic side. The laconic signals of the aeroplane spotting for her amused us greatly.

" You are right for direction and elevation."

The *Agamemnon* got busy.

" You are hitting."

The *Agamemnon* got busier still.

THE DIN OF ARMS 151

" Enemy running."

The *Agamemnon* congratulated herself.

" I am going home."

Friday, May 7th, was another heavy day ashore, and the French fought magnificently, gaining the desired ridge, but with great losses.

Some of us from the ship were lucky enough to watch in safety, from a rise two or three miles behind the firing line, a modern battle. It was intensely interesting, but curiously lacking in the elements of wild excitement and thrilling incident. What had we expected ? we wondered. Charges of the Light Brigade, storming of the heights of Dargai, or the Relief of Mafeking ? Of anything like any one of these longed-for items there was no sign at all.

A picturesque goatherd, with a lithe youthfulness in his step, shepherded a number of thirsty goats destined for the Indian brigade; farther off were groups of resting soldiers in twos and threes smoking cigarettes—Woodbines, their scent betrayed them ! Now and again an orderly galloped past, stretcher-bearers with the wounded slowly climbed the hill, and big A.S.C. waggons grated by filled with the helmets, accoutrements, and rifles of the dead and wounded. When an ammunition tumbril with six horses dashed along—really dashed—we felt we were touching the real thing at last.

But no. It was impossible at that distance, even with the continuous roll of rifle fire in our ears, to feel that we were near a real battle. Perhaps the flowers round about us forbade it. The yellow jessamine, three feet high, determined to come out green and bright in the midst of all the horrors; the gorgeous bronze-red poppies winding in crimson paths through a sea of blue salvia; and what the Japanese call "morning glory," and we know as the convolvulus, but pink only, trailing everywhere. There was also a pale blue, starry, flat flower about eight inches high, with spines sticking out under the petals, something like "love-in-a-mist"—as indeed, it would have been by that time had such a thing as love ever existed in the tragic Peninsula. Clouded yellow butterflies fluttered on slender wings above the flowers; swallow-tails, too, like tropical blossoms blown by the wind.

Below us the valley, with vineyards and cornfields spreading up the sides of Achi Baba, and in the nearer distance a good fir or two, seethed with smoke like a witch's cauldron. When we could

1. ON BOARD HOSPITAL SHIP "DEVANHA."
2. WOUNDED FROM THE SUVLA LANDING.

WOUNDED COMING IN-BOARD. HOSPITAL SHIP "DEVANHA."

THE DIN OF ARMS 153

see across it we marked the shells bursting in one continuous stream over the trenches of the enemy, the ship's shells being easily distinguishable from the British 18-pounders and the French ·75's, by the size of their explosions.

Between the rise where we stood and the firing line were thirty thousand British and a vast number of French. The whole valley and side of the hill was a warren of guns—one hundred and sixteen was the number given us of the British pieces alone. Yet not one was visible. Try as you would, it was impossible to locate them. You could walk within a few yards of a battery from the rear and not know it was there, and if you were sufficiently enterprising to make search from the front it was impossible to distinguish its presence except by walking into it.

Four Lancashire territorial battalions arrived that day, and were marched straight to the firing line and flung into the battle—our battle. Before this they had not seen a shot fired in earnest, and, without any process of breaking in, had to march across the open exposed to a hail of shrapnel ere they had the smallest chance of retaliating. It is the more to the credit of these battalions that they gave such a splendid account of themselves during the next few months of fighting and hardships.

In the evening the Anzacs made their historic attack towards Krithia. We were so cut off from Anzac that little news from there percolated through to our side of the Peninsula, and we were comparatively ignorant of the great deeds that had been enacted Gaba Tepe way. For the first time we were made aware of the fighting qualities of the Australians and New Zealanders, and somehow those of us who had gone down to the Australian sea in ships in days gone by felt the pride of race the Anzacs admitted in their coming. We recognized the strong claim of brotherhood this fighting together made upon us, and as the rifles rolled out the message of the taking of Krithia, of the driving back and then the holding of a forward position, the master-words of the immortal of whom the Australians have often heard stirred dimly in the brain: " We be of one blood, thou and I !"

The intensity of the fire round Krithia was soul-stirring. For fifty minutes hundreds, or without exaggeration thousands, of shells were dropped at this point from more than one hundred and fifty guns, naval and shore batteries. Still

THE DIN OF ARMS 155

no marked advance was possible. The defence was admirably planned, and the enemy maxims well hidden.

After fifteen days' fighting the Allies held a line across the Peninsula representing an advance of three miles from Cape Helles and about three and a half miles long. Heaven and the authorities alone knew what it had cost! Every yard of ground was entrenched by the Turks, and we were now down to a trench warfare in which gains and losses of terrain are reported in hundreds of yards after a day's severe fighting. The night attack was no longer so popular with the Turks— they had learnt their lesson.

Our guns were feeling a trifle warworn with constant use. A choke in the fore-turret 12-inch needed humouring—the A tubes were twisting and lengthening. We had a premature shell burst from the right gun of the fore-turret, which by the mercy of God did not kill anyone on board the *Albion* or on the beach, though pieces of shell fell all around. Some of the 6-inch guns were getting well worn also.

We changed places with the *Agamemnon*, and the *Lord Nelson* with the *Implacable*, which from the first had been responsible for X Beach. It was pleasant to know that the *Cornwallis* had gained a reputation off V Beach for work well done. We did not move far—just inside the Straits on a beat between De Tott's and the entrance to the Dardanelles. Our duties were to keep the Asiatic batteries in subjection and to be inside ship supporting the French troops, whose right flank rested on the cliffs touching the Straits.

We had an immediate welcome from a howitzer battery which suddenly opened fire on us in the midst of a peaceful afternoon watch when we were at anchor. Half a dozen rounds fell within fifty yards of the ship—a most unpleasant sensation. One could hear the shell screaming through the air a long way off, and it seemed as if one could tell exactly where the shot was going to fall as it culminated in the crash ! bang ! We weighed at once and cleared away the fore-turret, and then let them have a couple of rounds of 12-inch at the suspected spot. Later we, with the *Implacable*, stirred up some of the Asiatic batteries, or rather places where we thought batteries lay.

About this time Lieutenant Budgen, R.N., and his party returned to the ship from their wanderings among the transports, where they had

THE DIN OF ARMS 157

been disembarking men, horses, mules, guns, ammunitions, and stores, since April 25th. Their work had been lacking in the spectacular, but during the first five days they toiled the clock round. Lieutenant Madge, R.N.R., another absentee, came back to us with his little lot. He had been in charge of a beach party responsible for the clearing of lighters and the hundred and one boats which landed the army and its stores on V Beach, and from the great day of landing had lived in the *River Clyde*. Shelling or no shelling, the beach parties had to be on duty, and those running the boats were as often as not under fire. He told us of his experiences on the 25th April, when he went in to the beach twice, the first time without abnormal losses, and the second when only four men escaped unwounded out of twenty-three and ten were killed, including Midshipman Hardiman, who lived two hours after being hit.

In this series of glimpses at great happenings which, in their relation to each other and in their issue, are well known to us all, the form of our record could not be what it is if it did not deal with a compelling background in the stream of events—the care and treatment of the wounded.

There is no doubt but that at the commencement of the Dardanelles operations the R.A.M.C. arrangements were not equal to the demands made upon them, and this breakdown was not due to any slackness on the part of the medical officers and orderlies who were on board individual ships—no body of men could have worked more devotedly. It was confidently expected that Achi Baba would be occupied within two days of the landing, and, this peak held, the Southern end of Gallipoli would have been free from shell fire, and base hospitals were to have been established on shore. As things turned out, no land bases could be formed and the wounded of necessity were brought from the firing line to the beaches, where often enough they had to wait some hours before they were taken on board the trawlers for transportation to hospital ships. These were soon filled to overflowing, and big transports were converted at a moment's notice into hospital carriers. The ships our Chaplain visited when it was his turn for Chaplain's guard were of this latter class.

He left the *Cornwallis* early one morning in the fleet-sweeper told off to take him round, and first went on board the *Southland*. Here were

THE DIN OF ARMS 159

the comparatively slightly wounded, of whom there were one thousand and eighteen, and among them all only forty cot cases, of whom not more than two were serious. The organization was excellent. There was no crowding, so many men being told off to occupy each space, and everyone had a ticket stating his deck, place of feeding, and whether he was to attend the first, second, or third dinner. The *Alaunia* was next boarded. Splendid work was being done by the Colonel in charge, a well-known Liverpool surgeon, and three assistants. None of them ever seemed to rest, and there were in the ship seven hundred wounded, of whom at least one hundred and fifty were cot cases. The slightly wounded were lying on mattresses along the upper deck verandas, and the worst cases were below.

To the *Franconia* next, a fine Cunarder. She had only been transformed into a hospital carrier the preceding day, and already there were nine hundred wounded on board, four hundred being cot cases, and more were arriving each minute, until every inch of space was taken up with one thousand six hundred wounded. To deal with this vast number were three surgeons, one dispenser, and twenty-five orderlies.

It is indubitably a fact that the majority of wounded men after the first field dressing do not want further dressing for twenty-four hours, and only require warmth and rest; but a certain percentage of the extremely seriously wounded—and there were a number in the *Franconia*—required instant attention. It was impossible for so small a staff to cope with the work, despite the fact that every man in the ship, from the Captain down to the junior cabin-boy, lent a hand. The seamen were getting in the wounded and lowering them into the hold, and the stewards were supplying and distributing food.

So inadequate did the Chaplain consider the number of doctors on board that he asked the senior medical officer if he should take a request to the Admiral to send naval surgeons to assist, and this offer was readily accepted; so, leaving the *Franconia* after dark, the Chaplain went on board the flagship, and being taken to the Rear-Admiral, detailed what he had seen. At once a steamboat was called away, and the Rear-Admiral went, taking Mr. Peshall with him, to the *Arcadian*, where the Headquarters Staff of the R.A.M.C. were living.

The upshot of the interview was that a doctor

THE DIN OF ARMS 161

from the *Euryalus* was sent to the *Franconia* that night, and the following day each big ship was told to send one to help in the hospital ships. Surgeon Galloway was lent from the *Cornwallis*.

The wounded throughout the whole campaign were magnificent in the unflinching manner in which they bore untold sufferings, and patient beyond belief. The one thing they always wanted was cigarettes, and quaintly enough they would tell the Chaplain very often how glad they were to see someone in civilian clothes. Such a happy change, they thought.

May 10th was a particularly lively day; the enemy began shelling at cockcrow, and as usual we replied, a duel which continued on and off for hours. The *River Clyde* was hit twelve times, and the beach was not a healthy spot to go near; but nobody was killed and little damage was done—another proof, if proof were needed, of the ineffectiveness of shell fire unless concentrated.

During the next few days three thousand six hundred and fifty French wounded were officially returned as having passed through V Beach. The Senegalese about this period were removed from the Peninsula, as, though excellent in attack, they were of little value in trench work. Four Turkish destroyers were reported as being at Chanak, just beyond the Narrows, and thereon hangs a tragic tale which was unravelled a couple of nights later. Intermittent fire from the Asiatic batteries livened the hours, some heavy shell coming from the battery near the Suan Dere River.

Our casualties were mounting up—the total since the landing was close on twenty thousand. On May 9th an armistice was arranged to allow the Turks to bury their dead in front of the British lines, but when it was seen they were improving the shining hour behind the cover of thick bushes by placing maxims in position the truce came to an end.

Rear-Admiral Wemyss came on board and expressed satisfaction with our methods of dealing with the Asiatic batteries. He asked if the men were tired and would like a rest. No, everyone wanted to be useful, all hands were as fresh as the paint of olden days. We had no paint to speak of now! Every ounce had been chipped off to lessen the danger arising from fire. The sides grew rustier every day. Time had indeed worn us into slovenry, " but, by the Mass, our hearts were in the trim."

## THE DIN OF ARMS

Some interesting documents were distributed round the fleet, translations of Turkish despatches which had fallen into the hands of the military. They showed how strongly Morto Bay had been held, and also gave the information that the Turks had an army corps in Gallipoli and another at the head of the Gulf of Xeros.

"TURKISH DIVISIONAL ORDERS.

"*7th April.*

"The 2nd regiment will send one of its Battalions to the Tekke Burnu–Sedd-ul-Bahr line. This battalion must place its reserves among the trees in the Dere; the other battalion will place its maxim gun company between Keste and Sedd-ul-Bahr in a suitable position in reserve. These battalions will send out one section towards places favourable for the enemy's disembarkation to the north of Tekke Kin, also towards Morto Bay and Dornous Bay. The defence and protection of this zone being very important, they will meet the enemy's attempt to disembark from the north and from Morto Bay with searching fire, and if necessary will pass to the attack with the bayonet with all their forces."

"REGIMENTAL ORDERS No. 181. ADDRESSED TO O.C. No. 7 BATTALION, 26TH REGIMENT.

"KRITHIA,
"*25th April.*

"*Article* 10.—Both the field and howitzer batteries will be so placed as to fire against Morto Bay and the well between Sedd-ul-Bahr.

## 164 THE IMMORTAL GAMBLE

"*Article* 11.—If a counter attack be made against the enemy the O.C. Division announces in his orders a conviction that a very serious disaster will be inflicted on the enemy in the assault which he has made by sea up to now. This conviction is strengthened by the endurance and success which has been displayed by our soldiers under the shells of the enemy's fleet off Sedd-ul-Bahr. Everybody may be confident that however many troops the enemy may try to land, and however heavy the fire from his guns, it is absolutely impossible for the enemy to succeed. Let officers and men be convinced that there is no possible going back when the safety of the Fatherland is at stake and the glory of victory is upon us. Officers commanding units should act with the greatest coolness, and must pay special attention to not calling on their reserves prematurely.—*Signed by O.C. 26th Regiment, Bimbaslio.*"

" EXTRACTS

" No. 1.—The password to-day is ' Chak.'

" No. 6.—To O.C. No. 3 Battalion. The 25th Regiment is coming up; hang on. Captain has been killed and the Company has suffered incredible losses.

" No. 13.—The enemy's infantry is taking cover at the back of Sedd-ul-Bahr gun defences, but the rear of these gun defences cannot come under fire. It is certain that the enemy has landed at Sedd-ul-Bahr; and with the twenty to twenty-five men I have with me it will not be possible to drive the enemy off with a bayonet charge, because I am obliged to spread my men out. Either you must send up reinforcements and drive the enemy into the sea, or let us evacuate this place, because I see it is certain they will land more men to-night. Send the doctors to carry off my wounded. Alas ! Alas ! My Captain ! For God's sake send up reinforcements, because hundreds of soldiers are landing. Hurry up. What on earth will happen ? My Captain ! My Captain !—*From* ABDUL RAHMAN."

## THE DIN OF ARMS

About this time, too, a fragmentary diary kept by a German officer was picked up. He was a war correspondent maybe, a pedant anyhow, for when translated his page ran: " In so far as my studies in geography were directed to the knowledge of the people who dwelt in Turkey, and could be prosecuted at my writing-desk and in European Universities, I had brought them to such a point as to consider myself capable of forming an idea of the growth of at least some few rough features of the entire campaign."

How nationally characteristic both in plan and thoroughness ! It reminds one of the story of the essay on camels demanded of three students, English, French and German, who went up together for an examination. The Frenchman hied himself forthwith to the nearest Zoo, and through impeding bars investigated as much camel as he could see, that evening committing to paper in expansive and flowery language, with a million diversities, all he thought of " ce quadrupède magnifique, le navire du désert." The Englishman took a ticket for the nearest get-at-able spot where one may confidently expect to find the camel at home, and there studied the practical side of camel culture, making copious notes the while. The German retired to his room, and shutting himself in with every ancient and modern book, treatise, and memoranda on camels —and they are very many, almost as numerous as books on Spain—proceeded to read, mark, learn, and inwardly digest every word of them. In the course of three or four years he was so completely soaked in camel-lore that before he had even completed a monumental essay on the results of his investigations prior to going out and verifying them, he was rated as the world's greatest authority on camels.

# CHAPTER IX

THE LOSS OF THE "GOLIATH"

FOR the first time in many weeks the Turkish searchlights were not busy on the night of May 13th—only two minute beams could be seen far, far up the Straits, much higher up than usual. It was a significant change. There was no moon, and the darkness was Eastern in its intensity— it would have been difficult, if not impossible, to see a torpedo boat at one hundred yards' distance. Critical appraisement of the chances of an attack—suspicion had been aroused by the Turkish torpedo craft reported about Chanak— forced the conclusion that it was a likely night, and special warning was given to the look-outs and guns' crews of the *Cornwallis*. As usual, there was our destroyer patrol above De Tott's, where a little to the south lay the *Goliath*, acting as flanking ship to the French line, with the *Cornwallis* astern of her, about a mile away in Morto Bay.

The First-Lieutenant was on watch from 11 p.m. to 1 a.m., and left the bridge about twelve minutes after 1 o'clock. When winding his watch in his cabin, he noticed the time was 1.17, and almost immediately afterwards felt rather than heard two distinct shocks, so faint, however, that he took the sensation to be pumps discharging or the engines turning, as they occasionally do when the ship has steam at short notice.

The shrill pipe, " Watch fall in !" followed by " Away all boats !" spread the news of some disaster, the magnitude of which was not at first realized.

Lieutenant-Commander Courage was on the bridge, and his account of the torpedoing of the *Goliath* was that there was no more sound of an explosion than would have been caused by the firing of a big gun. He heard two detonations, but men nearer the water line in their bunks and hammocks heard three.

Black smoke rose in no great clouds, and it was some minutes before anyone realized that the *Goliath* had been torpedoed. Only as the cries of men in the water floated to us through the darkness was the tragedy understood. The rifle

## THE LOSS OF THE "GOLIATH"

fire from the trenches was continuous, and it was difficult to hear clearly.

The Captain, sleeping in the fore-bridge cabin, was awakened at once. "Clear lower deck!" was sounded and the general alarm rung. Searchlights were switched on, and all hands were engaged in lowering and manning every available boat.

By this time there were pieces of wreckage off our port beam drifting down rapidly, and on all manner of spars and bits of wood men, clearly visible in the rays of the searchlights, were hanging desperately and hailing the ship.

One would imagine that after having seen hundreds of dead and wounded one would be inured to shocks of all kinds, but nothing we had experienced affected us so profoundly as the sight of these men, swept past in the darkness on a five-knot current, and the sound of their voices rising from the water.

The *Goliath* had gone! The sickening realization that we had lost another ship was merged in a thousand other whirling thoughts—in her sudden passing was the difference between the death of a friend and that of an utter stranger.

Our steamboat was first away, followed by the

two cutters and then the pinnace. Altogether our boats rescued 56 men, but out of the *Goliath's* crew of 750 only 183 were saved, including 21 officers. The current was so strong it was impossible for anyone to swim to the *Cornwallis*— the nearest man got to within two hundred yards, and nobody was saved by coming on board direct.

Signalman Beall, R.N.V.R., gives the following account of what he saw on watch and the rescue work:

" I was on watch on the bridge, when there was a loud explosion, which I took to be the firing of a very heavy gun, and at the same time I noticed large clouds of smoke issuing apparently from the funnels of some craft to the right of the *Goliath's* position. About two minutes later there came to us cries, which all thought were the Frenchmen exulting in a victory of some kind, and it was not for some minutes that we could distinguish the words ' Ship ahoy !'

" I was sent away in the first picket-boat in case a signalman might be wanted, and we at once went to the rescue of anyone we could see. We had to work at slow speed, as our searchlights and those of other ships only served to make the darkness more terrible, and we were afraid of running down the men struggling in the water. I never want to have a more heartrending job! It was simply awful while picking up one man to hear another not twenty yards away shouting, 'Picket-boat, help! Quick! I am nearly done!' when we knew that the current was sweeping him downstream into the darkness. Our boat picked up thirteen men in all, and without exception every man as he was hauled aboard muttered a fervent, and I am sure perfectly pious, 'Thank God!' The poor fellows were terribly cold, and I soon dispensed with my jersey and greatcoat, and all the boat's crew were stripped to a minimum by the time we got back to the ship. But tragedy cannot damp the spirits of the matlow. Not ten minutes after one man had been hauled on board the picket-boat, he turned to his mate, and said: 'Just my luck! I lose deal again; I only did my dobeying (washing) last night.'

"After cruising round for some time without finding any more survivors, we returned to the ship."

The officer of the watch was one of those who came on board us after being rescued by one of our boats. The first thing to raise his suspicion that an attack was impending was the faint outline of a strange craft creeping along inside the European shore. Instantly he flashed the night challenge at her, and received no reply. The mysterious boat then shot ahead at full speed, and the *Goliath*, which was at anchor, had only time to fire two or three rounds from a 12-pounder, when the first torpedo hit her under the port anchor bed. The enemy T.B.D. crossed the bow, turned to starboard, and put a second torpedo under the fore-turret and a third under the cutter's davits amidships (both on the starboard side), and dashed off into the darkness, slipping past our patrol.

The *Goliath* heeled over to starboard, and before most of those below could reach the deck turned bottom up, remaining thus for a couple of minutes, when she sank bows first.

Tugs and trawlers and boats were cruising in every direction trying to pick up survivors, many of whom were carried on the strong current for a great distance. A Midshipman, upheld by a Gieve safety waistcoat, was picked up still breathing two days later, but his exhaustion was such he could not be brought round.

From the point of view of a destroyer officer there is no doubt but that the attack was skilfully

## THE LOSS OF THE "GOLIATH"

carried out by the (as we heard afterwards) German in command. It is probable that the entire crew of the T.B.D. were Teutons, not Turks.

The *Cornwallis*, the flanking ship, was in a position to court disaster, and her providential escape was the second we considered her to have experienced since the commencement of the Dardanelles operations. We might easily have been stationed where the *Goliath* was, or the destroyer might have passed her in the thick darkness and come on to us.

We got under way after we could render no further assistance, and stood out to sea, but returned to our post in the forenoon; and as though we had not undergone enough excitement for one day, the *Cornwallis* was heavily shelled, seven big projectiles falling close alongside. They were all 8-inch or more, but by this time we were so used to having shells fired at us and dropping close that it would have come as a surprise had one landed on board. In the afternoon we were engaged again in silencing a battery on the Asiatic shore that was shelling V Beach and the *River Clyde*. We knocked them out, and they brought up another battery next day. And so it went on.

At dark we left for Mudros, and on our way sighted a strange-looking craft steaming fast with all lights out. She refused to answer the night challenge satisfactorily, so we started in chase of her, and pursued her for two or three hours, but not being much of an ocean greyhound the *Cornwallis* failed to overhaul the mystery ship or find out what she was. Probably one of our own merchantmen, frightened out of her life, or a transport under definite orders to stop for nothing. Such a procedure had its dangers, as we fired three rounds from the 12-pounder at her.

The *Queen Elizabeth* left the fleet, and we did not expect to see her again off Gallipoli. With the Admiralty orders concerning the care of the valuable unit, it was probably with more relief than regret that the Vice-Admiral, who hoisted his flag in the *Lord Nelson*, saw the latest super-Dreadnought depart. The consoling formula which invariably followed on the loss of each one of the old ships sunk, " of small military value," would have been useless as a palliative where the *Queen Elizabeth* was concerned. By no possible feat of political legerdemain could an accident to Her Majesty be offered to the public as a blessing in disguise.

To hark back a little—the general reader is no doubt pondering over what "matlow" means, and speculating whether any French *marins* were on board the *Goliath*. Our men do not call themselves by the names bestowed on them by the public, "Bluejacket," "Jack Tar," and the rest. They are matlows or matlos, an age-old term, and common in our navy for many years before the *entente* introduced us to the French *matelôt*.

Curious how words may, as that master of them once said, "become alive and walk up and down in the hearts of their hearers"! And perhaps the seaman, more than any other man, is wholly in thrall to the lure of words and names. He hears so many in strange ports, almost they seem to blow on the wind for the catching, and he, adapting them to his needs, keeps them by him, like counters to be reckoned with.

Words come into fashion suddenly in the navy. Some are promoted from the lower deck, others gain a part of their lustre from ages of Ward and Gun-room attrition. Just at present the key word is "stunt." Everything is "stunt." Its American taskmasters wouldn't know the poor little syllabic slave in its new gyves, for when it set forth, an ambitious, industrious, picturesque Transatlantic tool, it expressed something, it had a meaning. It has none on board ship. The war is a "stunt," church is a "stunt," watch-keeping is a "stunt," meals are "stunts," stations are "stunts," beach parties are "stunts"; and so all-conquering "stunt" goes forward, until Time, greatest of innovators, provides a substitute. It is not easy to make a mariner of "stunt"!

As a rule the naval man's time-worn allusions have, if you take the trouble to probe them to their philological depths, an origin and meaning, for the sea is a character in his life rather than the circumstance it is to the technical writer, who showers nautical words and knowledge upon us to our bewilderment. We know them for nautical words, certainly, but equally we know they are technically nautical words for the use of landsmen, and that the mariner has a vernacular of his own. There is a great difference between technically nautical and nautically technical expressions. Would the average seaman, for instance, supposing he wielded a ready pen, word-weight the recounting of a ship-wreck as Falconer did in the celebrated poem ? A seaman—though Falconer

CORN-THRESHING WITH OXEN AND SLEDGE, ISLAND OF LEMNOS.

SUNSET IN MUDROS HARBOUR.

## THE LOSS OF THE "GOLIATH"

knew something of the sea—would give you the disaster in a far more catapultic style.

It was remarkable how the island of Lemnos had changed during the month. Summer in these Greek islands is like a magician, who changes as with a wand of gold the face of the earth in the twinkling of an eye.

The crops, it seemed, were planted, grew up, and were harvested in the space of three months. The methods of cultivation were the methods of Biblical times. Strange that a people prehistoric enough to use archaic ploughs and such an obsolete system of corn grinding should be the romanticists of the world! Romanticists are always adventurers, as the old Greek legends tell.

We had seen the wooden plough of the country, drawn by yoked oxen and the proverbial ass, turn the ground; had watched a figure, who might have stepped straight out of a Millet canvas, throw the grain broadcast with both hands; and now the whole place was harvesting, down to the youngest inhabitant, who lay on his back in a corn stook, gazing at the brazen sky with the eye-power of a young eagle. The sickles used were the oldest fashioned of implements; if Noah harvested, he harvested with just such others.

A little later we saw the ears of corn, strewn in a circle over a hard pounded piece of ground, and the yoked oxen treading out the grain. Sometimes a woman bumped about on a balk or sledge studded with flint teeth towed by the bullocks over the corn ears. Round and round they trailed, she trying to keep her place on the unstable perch in her desire to add her weight to the threshing scheme, and the beasts going like a clock which needs winding.

Some three hundred Turkish prisoners were at work making roads and digging foundations for French store-houses. The dusty little town was trodden out to its uttermost areas, and only after quite an exploration now could one reach "the country."

In the High Street the majority of the booths had vanished, since the sale of spirits was forbidden, but there was a brisk business of all kinds doing. When all Europe was fighting, destroying, and all the time consuming, this was the islander's opportunity, and he was going to improve it.

Wise people, when they have not been killed, have always prospered at the expense of the fighters.

## CHAPTER X

THE COMING OF THE GERMAN SUBMARINES

BACK again after two days, when we took the place of the *Implacable* off X Beach, which was always under heavy fire.

Boy Pearson and Boy Baker were promoted ordinary seamen for gallantry under fire at De Tott's landing; and we heard—these little items made up the interests of the ship's company just then—of the sending back to Alexandria of one thousand six hundred Indian troops, and this in no way for incompetency or disaffection. An order from home set forth that no more than a certain percentage of the troops in the Peninsula were to be Mohammedans, and it was a question whether the Egyptian pioneers were to remain or the Indians. They were all of the greatest value, but the former could not be spared, as there were no other men available with the same kind of training, and after unavailing protests from officers and men the one thousand six hundred Indians departed for the base.

Rumour reported German submarines in the Mediterranean. There never was such a place as Gallipoli for the speedy circulation of all sorts of reports!

> " The flying rumours gather'd as they roll'd,
> Scarce any tale was sooner heard then told;
> And all who heard it made enlargements too;
> In every ear it spread, on every tongue it grew."

Alas! this latest chronicle, the first intimation we had of what was to become a deadly peril and the source of constant anxiety, proved only too true.

The Chaplain buried a petty officer from the *Goliath*, whose body had been found near X Beach —another indication of the extraordinary vagaries of the currents. The 3 to 5 knot stream coming out of the Straits was frequently deflected from its course by some counteracting influence, with the result that there was a current which swept objects completely round the foot of Gallipoli until they fetched up anywhere in the Gulf of Xeros. No two ships, though they lay close together, were ever seen swung in the same direction. And there was no mention of these remarkable currents in any of the charts—in fact, the whole of the survey work of the islands and mainland, as well as on the sea, was most inaccurate and untrustworthy. Commander (afterwards Captain) Douglas was responsible for a complete change in this direction; long before the landing he was working continuously from small boats at night, taking soundings all along the beaches and sea coast. And talking of surveying, it was, as the *Daily Wail* would say, " amazing " how inaccurate and unreliable the original maps supplied to the ships were. We were allotted two of the country on both sides of the Straits from Kum Kale and Sedd-ul-Bahr to beyond the forts at the Narrows, and when reduced to a common scale the position of forts and fortified places as given on these two maps did not synchronize, and it was not possible to make out locations definitely. Among the maps published in the home papers it would have been difficult to find one in which the places marked coincided with local opinion. In fact, it seemed to us that very often the enthusiastic map-maker had rechristened and reappointed numerous slices of Turkish territory without previously informing the natives of the change.

The reports of the presence of enemy submarines in the Eastern Mediterranean grew and grew. Two were only a hundred miles off now, and travelling at express speed. As a set-off to this evil news our own E 14 returned from the Sea of Marmora after what must be described as a magnificent exploit. The work of getting up a place like the Narrows was of a nature unknown in the training of submarine crews; the possible difficulties could not be gauged beforehand, and there was no knowing what manner of obstructions, or how many, the Turks would lay down to protect the Straits against an attempt to penetrate the Sea of Marmora.

The first ship to get up and the first to come down, E 14 was the pioneer of all future successful submarine expeditions. She was away twenty-two days, during which time, in between constant chasings about and being fired upon, she sank two gunboats and two transports, one a very large ship. The *Torgut Reis* was sighted when there were no torpedoes left.

For this gallant exploit Lieutenant-Commander Boyle received the V.C., his officers the D.S.O., and the men the D.S.M.

Boyle told us of the kindly greeting bestowed

on him by the French Admiral. The Admiral, on board a T.B.D., steamed round E 14 with a band playing " God save the King," and then went on board the submarine, where he fell on Boyle's neck, and kissing him on both cheeks, called him, " You beautiful boy !"

This was Admiral Guépratte, who was well liked and admired by all of us.

Many stories of spies found on the Peninsula reached us, and there is no doubt but that a few clever spies schemed their way into the fighting line and on to the beaches. Some of them were Germans, dressed in the uniform of dead British soldiers; others were Greeks employed ashore. Large-hearted spies some of these latter, for they spied on both sides ! The Greek contractor furnished with a permit to sell tinned foods ashore was a wily one indeed, with his carrier-pigeons caged in the larger tins, all neatly labelled and looking as though they had never been undone since they left the cannery.

A carefully disguised Teuton in the trenches called out " Stop firing !" at an inopportune moment for him, and he was hit over the head with a spade by one of the crew of a machine gun. There was also the historic occasion when the

Munsters were misled during a night attack by a counterfeit Munster passing the order, "Do not fire on the French," the so-called French being really Turks.

Repeated cases of signalling from Sedd-ul-Bahr to the Asiatic batteries occurred. Midshipman Forbes told a story of the hot fire suddenly opened from the Asiatic side when the soldiers were landing at V Beach. The first shots fell wide, but the aim was at once corrected, and further shells fell in the middle of the troops. It was then seen that a flashing light was at work on the cliffs. False signals sent up from the British lines towards Krithia, and the answers, were often reported.

About this time, towards dusk on a sultry evening, the enemy opened the heaviest fire over a small area we had yet suffered. Gully Beach, which lay to the north of X Beach, was their point of aim, and with beautiful precision for a full hour from ten to twelve shells a minute, mostly shrapnel with some common shell, fell in a continuous stream.

How shall we describe the plague of flies! In the hot weather, with ports closed, picture us with the disgusting pests lying thick on every scrap

X BEACH.

A FRENCH GUN AT GALLIPOLI.

of food and wherever else they could find resting space. From the dead to the living the countless thousands wandered, and back again. It was a horrible thought. We tried covering our plates at mealtimes with squares of muslin, manipulating our knives and forks beneath; but, bless you! the flies were upsides of a simple dodge like that, and just waited for the withdrawal of the loaded fork, when down they pounced, pursuing the food until one's mouth closed upon it. Even then they occasionally chased it down!

The Gurkhas were reported to have effected a fine bit of out-manœuvring the wily Turk. Twenty-five of the hillmen worked themselves round the edge of a sea cliff, hanging on by their eyelids almost, to a position which gave them the opportunity of firing twenty effective rounds apiece. The Turks at once attacked the place from whence the shots came, only to find it deserted. The catlike climbers had returned to their own lines. Later they established themselves across a difficult gully. The initiative and individuality of the Gurkhas' methods, whether on patrol or pitted against snipers, equalled, if it did not surpass, all similar tactics on the Peninsula.

There was much rifle-fire at nights—attacks

of sorts, but not very serious efforts, and our whole line advanced eighty yards and the Royal Naval Division three hundred yards.

A more varied round of duties opened up for us, all round and about the Cape Helles end of the Peninsula, for the battleships took turns at the different stations for bombarding, flanking ships, and firing on the Asiatic batteries; the most strenuous post being the right flanking ship inside the Straits off Sedd-ul-Bahr. We had a couple of days as right flanking ship and did a lot of firing, making good shooting on the Asiatic batteries, registering 12 O.K.'s and the rest within a margin of fifty yards of the Turkish guns, as reported by aeroplane observers. As right flanking ship next day we came in for great attention from the Asiatic gunners, who made much better practice than usual, many shells falling close about us. At last a 4·9 shell marked "Lot 4,1910," with the British Government arrow mark, came through one of our cutters hanging on the davits, and burst as it penetrated, fragments only hitting the deck.

The news of a heavy attack on the Australian position at Gaba Tepe came through to us. The Turks, rumour had it, were repulsed with a loss

COMING OF GERMAN SUBMARINES 187

of seven thousand, of whom three thousand were dead, while our losses were but seven hundred and fifty. Lawrence, who visited the Australian lines, told us later that hundreds and hundreds of Turks were lying in front of them. We picked up three thousand rifles without much seeking. The Turks asked for an armistice in order that they might bury the dead, but really to collect the rifles or try some trick of attack, so the Anzacs picked up all they could before granting a suspension.

The soldiers had a daily paper called the *Peninsula Press*, printed at General Headquarters, and there was rather a good yarn in it describing how during an armistice a Turkish soldier picked up one of our bombs and was making off with it, when one of our men called out. A Turkish officer pursued the thief, and making him give up the prize, dismissed him with a kick. Then, with a low bow and many apologies, the Turkish officer handed over the bomb to us. The *Peninsula Press* added: " The burial proceeded easily, thanks to the correct attitude of the Turkish officers."

All we heard and saw for ourselves proved that the Turk is a much less savage person than his German master. The Turks never stooped to liquid fire—they fought for the most part like gentlemen. Towards the close of operations the Turks employed poison gas, but not very successfully. The refusal to meet us in the open was the evil influence of Germany " doing on them." At the bottom of their hearts they hated the mole-like tactics as much as we did.

Occasional surrenders of Turks continued—one day two hundred came in at a time, and when our men occupied the vacated trench they found a dead German officer with nineteen bayonet wounds in him. At a distance it was extremely difficult to pick out the enemy for what he was, so little difference was there between him and our own war-stained men. The Turkish uniform was a sort of grey khaki and looked like a thick, smooth flannel, but there were many shades of colour—anything they could get near the right thing.

We had orders to cover and support a minesweeper which was to go up the Straits and lay out nets off De Tott's Battery. There was always anxiety lest the Turks should set off floating mines from Chanak to strike the two flanking ships, and the nets were intended to catch any mines that might come down on the

COMING OF GERMAN SUBMARINES 189

current. The sweeper did her work splendidly, laying out six hundred yards of netting in twenty minutes under a heavy fire. Of course we drew the fire of the enemy right away, and they shelled us with both large and small stuff, but did not hit us. It was a glorious morning, and the water without a ripple was threaded by a dark purple riband which marked the strong stream rushing out of the Straits. To watch the three escort destroyers, silvered in the sun, cutting their way through the glassy sea was the prettiest sight in the world. They kept on passing and repassing gracefully as we steamed slowly up the Straits behind the mine-sweeper. Two shells fell ominously close to us and threw up a mass of spray one hundred and fifty feet high, which took on the most wonderful rainbow effects and breaks of transparencies through which the gold of a thousand sunbeams shone.

But each day was very like the last, and we walked through a lot of ammunition. The *Cornwallis* alone in the three months she had been engaged had fired over three hundred and eighty rounds of 12-inch, about three thousand five hundred of 6-inch, besides a large number of 12-pounders.

Inside the Straits again—seven hours of it at quarters. We were told to open fire on the Turks, who were reported massing troops in front of the French position, so blazed away for three hours on end at a spot we could not see, receiving signals from the shore to correct the aim after each round. Of course the Asiatic batteries commenced on us, and managed to hit us once after many shots. The shell went through the funnel casing at the foot of the after-funnel, and finally came to rest, without exploding, on the stokehold grating, where a stoker picked it up quite casually and took it on to the messdeck. He was just showing his prize to his messmates, when one of them seized it from him and brought it down into the flat, calling for the Master-at-Arms. "You may depend upon it," said that disciplinarian as he told the story afterwards, "when I saw what he had in his arms he found my tongue hotter than the shell he was carrying, and he moved up the hatchway smarter than he came down."

The shell was placed in a bucket of water, and was eventually bartered for a tot of rum.

About this time we acquired the much-prized trophy now set up on our quarter-deck. It is

## COMING OF GERMAN SUBMARINES 191

an inscribed stone taken from the gateway of Fort 1. We had long spotted it and marked it down for annexation, but everybody was too busy to make up a raiding party. One afternoon Midshipman Forbes came on some French soldiers busily levering down the heavy slab, and as his hopes of securing the desired relic dwindled, his powers of persuasion—and the persuasive bounce of a midshipman is a most compelling force, let us tell you—rose to great heights. Before long he had the sympathetic Frenchmen convinced that the *Cornwallis* had some mysterious right to the stone, and they helped to remove it and even transported it to the beach, from whence Forbes brought it off proper midshipman fashion ! The inscription is in Arabic and, translated, runs thus: " This Fort was built in the reign of His Majesty the Sultan Abd-El-Hamid Khan the Second, year 1303, by the energy of the Colonels, Officers, and Men of the 2nd Battalion of the Redif."

We possess another trophy in the shape of a rifle with a dirty bit of white stuff adhering. This we secured when the Turks surrendered in the trench at De Tott's. It was probably the first white flag shown by them at Gallipoli.

On Whit-Sunday we coaled and ammunitioned ship in Mudros, working through the hottest day we had yet experienced, and the day following the officers had a bathing picnic, the first of many, and the men a well-earned make and mend clothes.

On Tuesday, May 25th, just a month to the day since the great landing, the hints and rumours of the presence of enemy submarines in the Eastern Mediterranean were authenticated with grim reality. A signal came through that the *Triumph* had been sunk off Anzac, and we learnt subsequently that, though her nets were out, the torpedo went through them as though they were thread. She sank within ten minutes of being hit, with the loss of three officers and sixty-eight men. The Australians and New Zealanders felt her going down so keenly that they volunteered to subscribe a month's pay apiece towards the expense of salving her. She had done excellent work ever since the landing, and was always ready with her guns or anything she had on board to help. If the joint Gallipoli operations have done nothing else, they have cemented the strongest of bonds between the Navy and the men of Anzac, which cannot fail to be another link in the chain of that fuller co-operation and understanding which all of us hope will be the outcome of the trials through which we have passed. And further, as was noted by the Australians themselves, any jealousy that might have been in existence before the war between Australia and New Zealand, and even between the individual states of Australia, had disappeared. Men who had proved their worth as the men of Anzac proved it find no room for the smallnesses of jealousy. They had been too near death together, and the unity which the new-coined name A N Z A C implies was established on the strength which each man from overseas found in the other.

The *Cornwallis* received orders to sail from Mudros at 7.30 on the evening of the day the *Triumph* was lost, and as we went out of harbour we met the big ships that had been on patrol returning to safety at full speed.

It was with mixed feelings that we made our way into the open, and there were few of us who had not on their persons or somewhere conveniently near at hand life-saving collars or belts.

We anchored off Gully Beach in the early morning, and at once nets were got out and every boat in the ship was lowered and moored astern, while the steamboats patrolled to seaward and we waited in momentary expectation of the thud. We had thought that some form of protection would have been provided in the way of a destroyer or trawler patrol, but we were left to our own devices, and the day passed without any sign of a submarine. It was with some relief that we received orders that afternoon to retire to Kephalo, in the island of Imbros, a subsidiary base some ten miles off, and we were thankful to have reached harbour without mishap, when the following morning brought us the news that the *Majestic* had met with the same fate as the *Triumph*, being sunk with the loss of forty-eight men.

We looked upon this catastrophe as the third of the three providential escapes which the *Cornwallis* had from being sunk all standing. Most probably the submarine, after sinking the *Triumph*, skirted round the southern end of the Peninsula and took refuge near Chanak. The morning afterwards she came down the Straits, and by chance we were not off Helles to be torpedoed. The *Majestic* lay conveniently handy, and though she was surrounded by small craft the German managed by what must have been a skilful attack to drive her torpedo home.

At the same time it must be remembered that both the *Triumph* and *Majestic* were at anchor, and the feat was no great one in either case. Still, it added to the heavy toll the enemy submarines had taken of our ships in other waters. And the reason is not far to seek. The submarine has grown up lately, and in manœuvres it was never the thing for small craft like T.B.D.'s and submarines to score off the battle-fleet, and so trial schemes never provided much scope; or else the minor successes of submarines were discounted or rules made that limited their chances.

And so we went on in our content, thanks to the all-powerful influence of the battle-practice return and the wisdom of Whale Island, which affected the idea that the percentage of hits to misses of torpedoes would be small. The cost of torpedoes expended by loss in practice was another limitation. Ah, well! we are learning our lesson, but at a cost of men and material.

Certainly these Germans were a day late for the Dardanelles fair. The army was well established, and no power on the sea or under it could prevent us supplying men and stores.

## CHAPTER XI

### IN HARBOUR

" Out of this nettle, danger, we pluck this flower, safety."
*Henry IV.*

IMBROS is perhaps the most beautiful of all the Greek islands, with its delicately etched outlines and masses of emerald green streaking off into the purple hills. The hills rise everywhere, and from the summit of a not far away peak the bursting shells from the Turkish guns at the back of Achi Baba could be distinctly seen with the aid of good glasses.

In between thinking out schemes for net defence in tropical weather, with no awnings up and the ship's sides red-hot and the atmosphere of Hades below, some of us walked to the horizon of the nearest hills. The rocks hereabouts were of a stone like marble, with radiant lights and veinings twisting through.

What had they done in Imbros with all the feminine inhabitants of a reasonable age, we wondered? There wasn't one between ten and forty, though many under and over that, and the most lyrical babies in the world.

The native dress appeared to be worn by the very poor only or by people living in the inland villages in little houses of wood and stone (wood mostly because of the earthquakes), tucked away behind the shoulders of the hills well out of sight of the pirates who up to quite recently raided all the islands as a regular thing.

Every kind of beetle and grub resided in Imbros, yellow and blue beetles, buff-coloured spiders big as tennis-balls, with enormously thick legs, and centipedes seven inches long.

A centipede first introduced the Pessimist to Alcide.

It was in the blank moment of his despair, when the centipede stood guarding a wooden bridge Horatius-wise, and gaping in the horribly human way centipedes have, that, quick as the god from the machine, appeared his saviour.

Never was a man so thoroughly abreast of a situation. With a sharp rounded spade the old Greek cut the centipede in two, and both bits ran away.

"I will make it quite safe for you," he whispered

so that none should hear. "You shall find no centipedes in Imbros when next you come. Anywhere I hate to see a stranger put upon in my own country."

Alcide never said, "It can't be done," or "Whoever heard of doing such a thing as that!" He knew what he wanted to do, and did it right away. He was a maker of the bells worn by the goats of the island, a mender of boots, and incidentally a judge of men and a lover of art—as was shown by his appreciation of the Pessimist's water-colour sketches, which he held as a good critic should, upside down.

Alcide wore the picturesque national costume of white stockings and rawhide shoes, black knickers with the seat hanging in an artistic bag far below his knees, a loose white shirt, an old scarlet cummerbund and a sort of cross between an Eton jacket and a bolero of dark blue. His cap was nondescript, so can't be described.

We visited Alcide at his house, where he warned us he could offer little but the pleasure of his society. "But always I set one thing against another," he said thoughtfully.

He made a cigarette for each of us the while

the ladies of his household, children and veterans all, brought in a tray with a bowl of jam, a glass of water per man, and a glass of liqueur and spoon apiece.

You take a spoonful of jam, drink some water, and then sip the liqueur, with a bow to each member of the family, and chat awhile until it is time to go. Sometimes they do the jam-liqueur trick a second time, and during the proceedings the women-folk stand and cannot be persuaded to sit down. The jam of the country was home-made, really home-made, the sort that mother used to make; also the liqueurs, which are chiefly of brandy variety; but the jams are composed of all sorts of things, quinces, tomatoes, rose-leaves, and violets, in which you can see the whole violet. They are all very sweet, but the Greeks don't eat jam as we do, but just take a spoonful and then drink a little water.

To Madam Alcide we opened up a new range of vision, for we were the first English she had met at close quarters. " In Athens I have seen them now and then," she said, " carrying red Bibles, and running into all the old tumbledown places, but carrying red Bibles always."

For a brief time we remained in our secondary

base, hedged round by all manner of precautions, and then Mudros harbour was our refuge. The enemy submarines were still at large, and as conditions were it seemed to us Fate had cast the *Cornwallis* high and dry on the beach and that she would not see any more fighting. In a general way Fate does not lavish benedictions, and the grave air of our Pessimist, as well as his lugubrious predictions, intimated that he considered the situation a serious one.

A heartening buzz went round that we were shortly going to Malta for a refit, and we hoped there was truth in it—a change would do everyone good.

E. 11 came out of the Dardanelles late one evening. They were a long way off us, but our cheers reached them all right. They had achieved great things, and officers and men eventually received similar honours to those of the pioneer E. 14.

Now and again Fritz at the gates was signalled, but for all that some of our ships went out from time to time and did a bit of shaking up of the Turkish positions; but we were not of the lucky ones, and there was plenty of time for thought in those days of comparative inaction—the First-Lieutenant, who was engaged in getting ashore

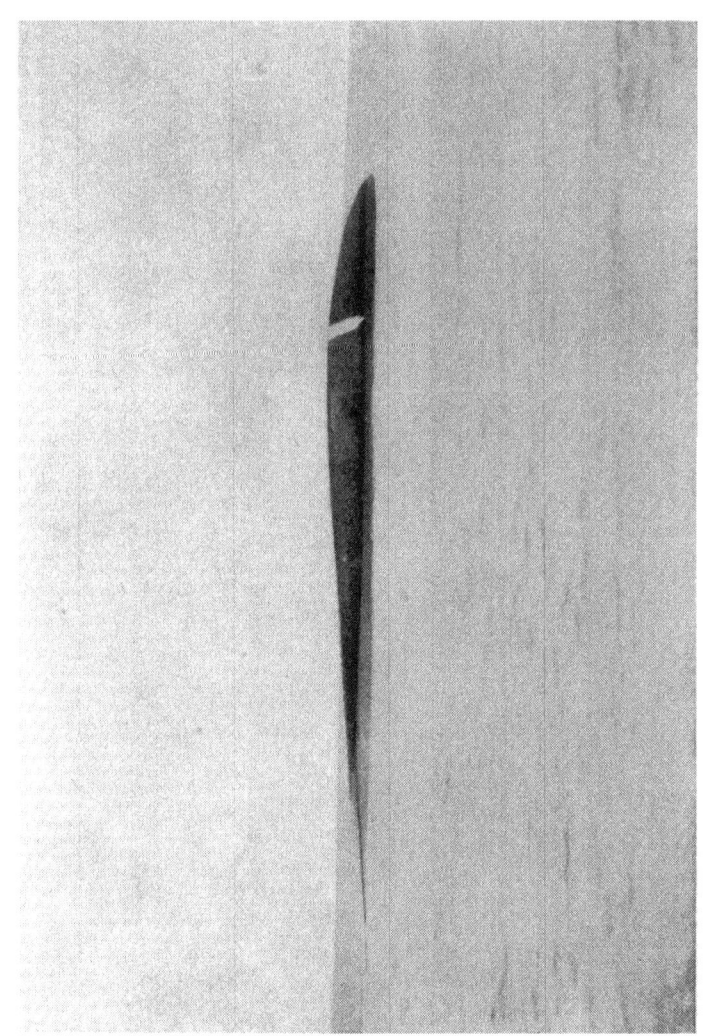

HIC JACET H.M.S. "MAJESTIC" (*page* 194).

A "REST" CAMP.

*Central News, Ltd.*

IN HARBOUR 201

machinery sent out for a distillery, says there is no "comparative" about them.

A great desire grew among the ship's company to show some recognition of the unbounded heroism of the soldiers other than the simple little acknowledgments we had hitherto been able to make. Supplies for the wounded most appealed to us, and a collection was made on board which resulted in the amassing of £44 6s. 10d. Instead of handing over the money to any official organization, we formed a purchasing committee, who were to lay out our hoard to the best advantage as soon as ever we got to Malta. This scheme proved the very best possible, for when we returned to Mudros in September from our refit we found that the wounded in the hospitals had little but the barest necessities, and in August they had lacked even these. It is no exaggeration to say there was scarcely a tin of food such as Benger's or malted milk in Mudros. Indeed, they were with difficulty procurable in Malta. And so our store of foods, cigarettes, tobacco, pipes, mosquito-netting, writing-paper and envelopes, soap, matches, games, tooth-powder and brushes, etc., came as boons and blessings to the British, Canadian, and Australian hospitals.

A yarn told us by a French naval officer who was ship's censor amused our own wielder of the blue pencil. He described an epistle written by a *matelôt* to his mother, which began by promising a cheerful and encouraging account of his surroundings. She was not to worry, not to concern herself in the least. Life on board was terrible: all day and all night the ship was under fire; shells dropped round her in hundreds and threw up cascades of water that swept the decks; submarines were reported every five minutes; mines went off at all points of the compass; " and then, dear mother, I recollected how the good Padre bade me look up to Heaven in times of danger. I looked up, and—le bon Dieu knows I speak but the truth—there were six aeroplanes dropping bombs upon us!"

Progress on the Peninsula was hung up for want of ammunition. Short of bombs and artillery ammunition as we were, we indulged in an attack after each arrival of supplies and then waited, Micawber-like, for more to turn up—a hand-to-mouth type of campaign. The Colonel of a Gurkha regiment described to us a successful attack on some trenches by his men, who had but thirteen bombs. Of course the Turks bombed out the invaders, who charged again and retook the trenches only to be bombed out once more. Five times that night the Gurkhas took this trench and were bombed out, and finally they held it.

Day after day as we saw the drafts of men leave Mudros in small craft for the Peninsula and we cheered the new arrivals; it made one's heart sick to think how many of them were going to die without the satisfaction of firing a shot or striking a blow for the country—the one thought that had animated them in all the weary months of preparation. So many lives, so little progress! So much stupid leading of good effort! Such wastage due to lack of ammunition! The Turks seemed to get ammunition enough for their guns, but they lost heavily in every attack and made no headway against our men at all.

We were busy making a hand-grenade on board —the *Cornwallis* patent. It was to burst on striking anything instead of having a time fuse. The Australians at Gaba Tepe had some men who could catch the Turkish bombs and throw them back—they reckoned they had three seconds in which to do it. Pretty smart work. But the *Cornwallis* bomb frustrated any such tactics, as it burst wherever it struck. It was simple to make, and practising with it most of us could throw it well over thirty yards, when the burst was excellent. It contained twenty-seven bullets, and we could not find a fragment of it anywhere. Half a dozen artificers could manufacture fifty a day—absurd, rather, when these things were wanted in myriads; but every bomb helped, and before long the growing fame of our patent caused the military to ask for a couple of thousand to be made by the fleet.

The First-Lieutenant was in charge of the big job of hoisting out of the *Port Lincoln*, with primitive appliances, and often with no appliances at all, 300 tons of machinery for a distillery plant, thrown in anyhow and despatched from England—two boilers of 9 tons each, six condensers of $6\frac{1}{2}$ tons each, three of $3\frac{1}{2}$ tons, two cases weighing $3\frac{1}{2}$ tons, and a dozen weights of over $1\frac{1}{2}$ to $2\frac{1}{2}$ tons.

A flat float was borrowed from the French—just the very thing—and the *Port Lincoln* was got alongside the *Cornwallis*, and work commenced. We had to hoist weights out of the hold with our main derrick, which did not reach the centre. What happened in the centre is another story!

The First-Lieutenant's plan was to build a

slipway and parbuckle the big weights off the float ashore, and land the small ones of one ton downwards by horse-boats; and the spot chosen was a beach where the water was not deep and the foreshore could be dug out to allow the float to be moored close in. It sounds ridiculously easy, but, as a matter of fact, this manipulating of such great pieces of machinery without even simple tackle was a job of work to be proud of. It was sultry, too, ashore, toiling hour after hour in the burning sun, and the working day was long— 7.30 a.m. to 7 or 8 p.m. On board the *Cornwallis* we had the quarter-deck awning spread now, and this helped to cool the ship somewhat.

The end of the distillery was not yet! The erection of the plant was on the programme and the landing of some three hundred tons of bricks. And if now and again some unappreciative rascal wondered why the military didn't attend to their own distilleries, or at least feign an interest in this one—adjective between " this " and " one " —you must forgive his querulousness: the sun was hot!

In early July the remains of the 29th Division were brought to Mudros from the Peninsula to a so-called rest camp—a bivouac of no tents and no comforts among the flies and dust. We invited on board for a couple of days at a time the officers of the South Wales Borderers, of whom there were but three of the original lot we had landed. Starting with twenty-six officers, they lost sixteen dead and twenty-two wounded, having had drafts amounting to twenty-nine. The last fight they were in was on June 28th, when a good advance was made. All had the same yarn to spin— trenches attacked without adequate artillery support, few bombs, shortage of ammunition. Time and again they had the Turks on the run, and were unable to follow because our guns were silent. Reinforcements dribbled in, and were shot down a few days or less after arrival before the men were accustomed to new conditions.

If there was no word of commendation to be said for the direction of affairs, there was the one bright spot in the magnificent fighting of the officers and men in the attack and in the trenches. They were splendid.

Proclamations advising immediate surrender were dropped in our lines from Turkish aeroplanes. " With the help of your navy you managed to land, but since the submarines arrived your ships have deserted you, and are at Lemnos afraid to move. You will be well treated if you surrender before you are all killed."

The advent of the monitors gave the answer. It was cheering to see them arrive, a most sensible type of craft, able to defy the submarine. Their coming would shake the Turks badly, and the guns of the navy would again lend the army valuable assistance.

We needed a Solomon on board to adjust a problem which presented itself. A marine saved from the *Majestic* was sent to us for punishment. He had been rescued by a Greek boat and taken to a port in Lemnos, where he got drunk and was arrested. His name, he said, was William Brown, a homely, familiar name enough, but not his own according to one of our marines, who identified the delinquent as one Trowbridge; and oddly enough the man's shirt was so marked. Two other marines came along and backed up the first, but in spite of them all the mystery-man maintained he was Brown and the victim of a cruel misunderstanding. He was plain Brown, he said, and had bought "the inconclusive shirt"—he used very grand and extremely descriptive language —at a sale of deserters' effects. Trowbridge had deserted.

We had nobody from the *Majestic* to solve the puzzle, and there the matter stood. Was the man Brown or was he Trowbridge ? And what motive could he have for concocting the deserter yarn ? One of our lieutenants saw the elements of a story in it, a plot with a reason for the change of name, a story bound, he thought, to wring £20—or was it £50 ? we forget—from a magazine editor on the lookout for a good thing; and the ingredients were mixed up forthwith: the sinking of the ship, the rescue by the Greek boat, the arrival in the Greek village, the reception by a lovely Greek maiden, the treating by a Greek rival, the casting into prison, and then the loss of identity. The main thing, the author said, was to forget William Brown, to picture instead a hero of romance head over ears in love with the beautiful Greek maiden, a hero who simply had to annex the name of a shipmate whom he resembled in order to evade the attentions of some difficult-to-lose plain and unattractive lady at home. But that was our difficulty. We could not forget Brown. His was the type of English beauty impossible to blot from the memory.

E. 7 returned from the Sea of Marmora, where she did splendid work. Her bag was one destroyer,

LOADING PATIENTS INTO HOSPITAL SHIP FROM PICKET-BOAT.

THE ROUGH HILLS OF GALLIPOLI.

IN HARBOUR 209

eight steam vessels, seventeen sailing vessels, and an ammunition train blown up. She also shelled Constantinople—or, rather, some powder works there. She was away three weeks, and had some narrow escapes, being caught in nets more than once. The sailing craft she sank by gunfire, likewise some of the small steamers.

Three months from the day of the great landing, and we were very little advanced since the first fortnight. One could say we had killed and wounded three times as many Turks as we had lost of our men, and one did say so often as a consoler. But things were moving. A change was to come over the spirit of the ugly dream. Men and material in great volume arrived, and the arrangements for a landing which had greater promise than the first went forward systematically.

The secret of the throwing ashore of two divisions at three spots at Suvla Bay, to the north of Anzac, was well kept, and the Turks were fairly surprised. The operation took place at night, from a special type of motor barge sent out in large numbers from home, supported by the monitors and cruisers fitted to resist torpedo attack; and the direct object of the new landing on August 7th was to cut the communications of the Turks by forcing a way from the Bay of Suvla to the Dardanelles Straits, a distance of six miles from shore to shore. This would have made the whole of Gallipoli to the south untenable, and the Turks would either have been obliged to surrender at once or cut their way through.

About thirty thousand men also were landed at Anzac. They were to attack to the north-east the hills overlooking the Anzac position—*i.e.*, Chunuk Bair and Sari Bair.

At first complete success attended the adventure: hundreds of prisoners were taken and a good advance made, but when the effects of the surprise attack had worn off the initial prosperity turned into what was practically failure. The weather was terrifically hot, and the troops employed had few seasoned men amongst them. They drank their two days' supply of water in as many hours; the supply ran short, and there was no means of replenishment, but the main cause of the set-back lay in the lack of support which was given to the first attacking line. History repeated herself, for it was just the same at Krithia on April 28th.

So here there were thousands of troops avail-

IN HARBOUR 211

able who had dug themselves in near the shore and were not sent forward to relieve and support the first troops who had made the successful attack. It was generally said, and generally believed, that there were in the first instance only five thousand Turks opposing the landing, and we had twenty-seven thousand men engaged.

The Turkish official reports expressed surprise at the lack of enterprise shown by the English in pushing home the initial success. They gave as a reason that the humane enemy were too careful of their wounded, and looked after them to the detriment of their fighting efficiency.

Although the ship was entirely out of this landing, we supplied some seventy men as beach party and boats' crews for both Suvla and Anzac. Gunnery-Lieutenant Minchin was in charge of two trawlers engaged in putting troops ashore and evacuating wounded, and during these operations one of our picket-boats at Anzac got a shell in her engine-room which broke the main steam-pipe, with the result that an excellent leading-stoker, J. B. Calder, was so badly scalded that he died. All in the boat behaved with the greatest coolness, and Stoker Ade went down into the steam-filled engine-room and rescued Calder. For this he was promoted leading-stoker, and has since received a well deserved C.G.M. The repair of the boat was most cunningly carried out by Foster, shipwright, and a man from the *Venerable*, a matter of no small difficulty, as she was in deep water and it entailed working while swimming. The two shipwrights swam alongside with lifebelts on, and the boat's crew pumped for all they were worth. Foster took two or three nails in his mouth and, hammer in hand, submerged himself the while he put a patch on and drove home the nails, and his mate stood by holding him steady by the lifebelt. This process continued until the boat was watertight again.

F. Coles, A.B., was severely wounded on the beach at Anzac and died six weeks later. J. Day was also wounded. Midshipmen Last, Edwards, Forbes, and Weblin were ashore at Anzac for weeks, as was Lieutenant-Commander Drake, R.N.R., who did such excellent work that General Birdwood sent him, on rejoining the ship, a personal letter expressing regret that he was leaving.

The Commander was at Suvla, engaged in transport work, and those left in the ship knew mighty little of what was going on. We could hear the big guns sometimes, though fifty miles off, but not a word of operations ashore was given out in Mudros—all one learned one got from individuals. We gathered that the recent landing was a success " on the whole "—ominous qualification! Some of the stories that filtered through made one wonder if human life had any value at all. Our losses were great, twenty-five thousand or thereabouts, and the sufferings of the wounded indescribable.

The whole campaign looked like a series of blunders. We were muddling through, but at what a cost!

Joy! To Malta at last for a refit, and late August saw us alongside in the dockyard with scuttles open. Scuttles open! But if you have never lived with them permanently closed you cannot realize what those words mean. All officers had four days' leave and the men fifty-six hours. We had the club and cinemas for amusement, and flies and mosquitoes to add to the hilarity.

And Malta was a vast hospital.

## CHAPTER XII

OF DOING NOTHING

WE were back in Mudros by the middle of September, and the place looked the same as ever bar that the hospitals ashore had grown much bigger. Heavy rains had cooled and freshened the air of the none too healthy harbour, but the flies still had their own way with everything. The rest camps, " christened sarcastik " surely, continued to receive soldiers from the trenches, who merely changed the variety of their discomforts. Decent huts instead of tents were growing up at last—about time.

On September 26th we went to Kephalo as Senior Naval Officer's ship. Now we could hear the dull thud of the guns all day long, and the Peninsula was in sight once more.

Boilers positively haunted the First-Lieutenant ! There was a job waiting for him ashore in the form of moving a thirty-two ton specimen about two hundred and fifty yards. First it had to be turned and then hauled along, turned again and hauled off the road. Next a roadway had to be built to take the big weight over a swamp, and the triumphant workers viewed the success of the operation as an achievement—which it was. Thirty-two tons is no small weight, and shifting it two hundred and fifty yards in twenty-two working hours was not a bad performance. The military had only managed to move the boiler at the rate of ten feet a day. Another boiler of equal size stood waiting transportation—the supply seemed endless. But now the roadway was built and had stood the first test, a boiler could be shifted in one day's work. By the time the amateur boiler-shifter and his working party from the ship got through with the job, and had taught the one hundred and fifty Egyptian labourers not to be so amenable to each other's hints as to resting-places, they had had quite enough of these pilgrim-distilleries, and hastened away from the roll-call of any that might be remaining.

The papers from home gave us Sir Ian Hamilton's despatch published September 20th. Alas! it was history, not fiction. A record containing nothing of the strategy or tactics of battles; an epic of the gallant and repeated bravery of all the splendid fellows whose lives had been thrown away in achieving nothing but imperishable effort and renown. Most of the time described was our strenuous time, too; many of the events were under our eyes almost. One read and read. The despatch might have been that of a war correspondent well within his rights in making war spectacular—the public asks that he should.

Between the lines lay unwritten stories to wring the heart! Well, " Silence, if rightly timed, is the honour of wise men." The Gallipoli campaign left the wisest speechless.

A Captain of the K.O.S.B.'s, a Scotsman and a keen fellow, spent a night on board—how he did appreciate a cabin and decent living after four months of it in the trenches! He told us a story of brave effort, of two hundred men left out of nine hundred and no drafts to speak of, as the battalion was a Territorial one. On June 12th they lost five hundred out of seven hundred, but the fight was not even mentioned.

If only the attack in August had succeeded! That was the murmur everywhere. It was our

OF DOING NOTHING 217

one chance. Now it was on and on with the interminable trench warfare. We had the guns, and the Turks the best positions. There was considerable sickness among the troops, and fine weather could not much longer be counted upon, but a great deal had been done in the way of making landing-places and anchorages secure.

Ten days without letters provoked the horrible rumour that the mail ship, which was any ship coming from Malta or elsewhere, had been done in by a submarine, and we thought that not only had we lost our home news but all papers relating to the recent fighting in France. Fortunately it turned out to be another of the highly coloured reports indigenous to our part of the world, which is not to hint that the sense of embroidery is lacking elsewhere, but to draw attention to the highly specialized variety peculiar to Gallipoli.

All the while we were at Kephalo, from September 26th to November 12th, the distribution of the naval mails for, and from, the beaches on the Peninsula, Tenedos, Kephalo Air Station, the ships and innumerable small craft attached to ships and places, was one of the numerous jobs which automatically came our way, as being part and parcel of the Senior Naval Officer's ship.

There had been bitter complaints of the delivery —or, as detractors said, non-delivery—of the mails and of the thieving and breaking open of parcels; but from a naval point of view, considering the conditions under which we served, we, as a ship, had little to complain about. It is true that our parcels were often smashed to fragments, but there were few cases in which some portion of them did not arrive, and their dilapidations were more often than not the fault of the packers. The circumstances under which the mails were handled did not tend towards careful treatment, even if the sailor were as gentle with other people's mail-bags as he would be with his own household goods. What could be expected! Imagine a picket-boat alongside a trawler transhipping mails in a heavy sea, and the same picket-boat bringing those mails to the distributing ship in the same sea, only worse. It was a case of catch when you can and dump in a lull.

The wanderings of any one letter after leaving England and arriving on the beaches would not be uninteresting. If for Gallipoli beaches it would have been in more craft than most men board in a lifetime. Up to Kephalo in twelve

OF DOING NOTHING 219

different ships and boats, and to the beaches eighteen. The personnel on the beaches was constantly changing; officers and men left, some sick, some killed or wounded, some relieved, and their letters had to be forwarded. This entailed another dozen transhipments. Ships, also, were constantly changing their areas of work, and the much-abused mail-officer was expected (and generally came up to expectation) to follow each movement. Was it surprising that a minimum percentage of letters and parcels went adrift, or that some parcels were smashed?

In mid-October there was nothing of any consequence doing. The monitors shelled the Turks regularly, and a comparatively small amount of trench warfare was continually in progress, and mining and counter-mining. Sir Ian Hamilton was wending his way home, and our main interest just then was whether or no we were going to be allowed out of our net-protected harbour to take a turn at Suvla as bombarding ship. Kephalo is open to the north and Suvla to south and west, and as these are the usual directions of the wind both places are fairly uncomfortable.

The inaction at the back of the front was hard to bear, and though all sorts of little jobs occupied us, there was nothing doing, nothing to take hold of and count as of real moment. Work on the boilers—we wondered at last if all the Greek islands were strewn with haphazard distilleries— proceeded in spasms, and the man who sent thirty-two ton weights to such a place as Kephalo was consigned by the working parties to the nethermost region.

General Birdwood was living on board us, having taken over the command from Sir Ian Hamilton until such time as the new G.O.C. should arrive.

E. 12 came down from the Sea of Marmora, having sunk four steamers and thirty-two small craft. She was away forty days, and fouled a net coming down, a part of which clung so that it was necessary to dive two hundred and forty feet. The rest of the distance home was accomplished bobbing up to the surface and down again under heavy fire from the shore batteries.

It was decided to sink the S.S. *Oruba*, a ship familiar to many travellers, as a breakwater at Kephalo. This means of making shelters and protection from bad weather for small craft was in process at all the landing places on the open beaches. The half-submerged ships would last fairly well, and the procedure took less time and expense than building breakwaters. All valuable and useful articles which would be under water after sinking were removed, and most of us came off with some unexpected luxury. The Commander annexed a fixed bath, and bathed thenceforward in more than Roman splendour.

It was intended to try and sink the *Oruba*, preserving the engine-room and boiler-rooms intact, and she was to be submerged by flooding, not by ballast, as had been done with all previous ships. When everything was ready and the position decided upon, the old ship weighed and proceeded to get into position by the aid of tugs, her own anchors, and wires to the ships already sunk.

Three charges were placed; one of two and a quarter pounds of gun-cotton at the after-end of the shaft tunnel close against the ship's side, tamped in with asbestos packing, planking, etc.; another forward in the forepeak, of similar size, a hole being cut in the foremost bulkhead to allow the water to flow aft; and another in the ventilation shaft to the shaft tunnel, to allow the water to flow into the after-hold when the tunnel was filled.

Small charges were used to prevent blowing

away too much of the ship's side and flooding her unevenly, but those used were too small and only allowed the water to come in very slowly, which entailed keeping the ship in position accurately for a considerable time. Consequently at 4 a.m. the next morning the *Oruba* was still afloat, and the wind springing up, parted the breast wire and necessitated finishing the job at once. Charges of four and a half pounds were then placed in number two hold and under number four, allowing her to flood quickly. The rush of water, however, broke down the watertightness of the engine-room bulkheads and doors, and fires had to be drawn and the engine-room abandoned.

The work of fixing the *Oruba's* position and reporting her settling was carried out by the *Endeavour*, all else by the *Cornwallis*, and Lieutenant Budgen, R.N. was responsible for the placing and explosion of the charges.

The ship finally grounded with a small list at about 8 a.m. Attempts were made to salve certain fittings from the engine-room and her dynamo by the aid of divers, but the *Cornwallis* was suddenly ordered to sea, and the work had to be abandoned.

## CHAPTER XIII

### THE EVACUATION OF SUVLA AND ANZAC

ON November 28th we left Mudros at daybreak, to take up duty at Suvla under the worst weather conditions we had experienced. For three days it had blown a gale from the north, which rose at times to strength ten and never fell below seven. Snow covered the hills to the water-line, and the air in the wind was so cold that it was blowing like clouds of steam along the tops of the waves, the water being warmer than the air. On deck it was much below freezing, and the sufferings of the men ashore must have been terrible—we thought of them constantly.

Suvla is a big bay, with an entrance two miles broad, and the headlands on each side form an excellent lee except from the west. The length of the harbour is something under two miles.

Looking from the sea to the right centre is the hill Lala Baba, where the only opposition to the landing was met, and behind again, inland, the salt lake, which in summer is almost dry. It was in crossing this in daylight on August 21st that the Yeomanry suffered so heavily, and lost some one thousand five hundred men. In winter the dry basin turned itself into a sheet of water below the clear line of the snows, and left but a narrow strip of, say, half a mile of land between itself and the Anzac Cove, where the Australian–New Zealand Army Corps held a position on the sierras which rose from the shore. Still farther inland Chocolate Hill stood above the crests of waves of ridges curling over as if about to fall momentarily, and from this point all the naval gunnery as well as some of the military was directed. Our front-line trenches ran one thousand four hundred yards inland from Chocolate Hill after both sides definitely dug themselves in, and beyond, again, was the small Scimitar Hill, held by the Turks, which was the scene of much fighting and severe losses. Far inland Hill W., an enemy arsenal and burial-ground of many *Cornwallis* shells, mounted steeply to its three hundred feet of height. To the left of the ridged hills in a shallow valley are the two Anafarta villages reached by us at one period of the operations.

GENERAL BIRDWOOD ON BOARD THE "CORNWALLIS" (*page 220*).

LORD KITCHENER AT GALLIPOLI.

From the northern headland which gives the bay its name a hog's back hill runs east and west, and, rising from the point and sloping away north and south to the sea about three-quarters of a mile off on each side, ends in three knolls: Jephson's Post—so called from the exploit of Major Jephson, who here rallied the retiring troops—the Bench-Mark, and the Pimple, both held by the Turks.

Along the crest of the Jephson's Post ridge our front line rested on the sea to the north and stretched westward of Chocolate Hill. The whole region was a network of gullies and small hillocks dividing and uniting and playing hide-and-seek with innumerable boulders and secret places. Never before had Nature contrived a country more suitable for the sniping tactics of the defence.

When we arrived in Suvla Bay the troops were suffering from the effects of the sudden blizzard. Officers and men had no more clothes than they possessed in the heat of August, and following on the tropical thunder shower of the Saturday night, which flooded the trenches and drowned many men, came the frost and snow from the north. The firing trenches on both sides were evacuated for part of the time, and even the guns were silent. At least sixty of our men were found dead from exposure and physical exhaustion, and eleven thousand were evacuated to hospital ships as a result of the three days' reign of terror. The Turks, as we gathered from prisoners, who were plentiful at this time, were in no better plight. All who came in had great-coats, but their underclothing was in rags and incredibly dirty.

We found the *Glory* acting as S.N.O., and the *Prince George*. We relieved the former.

The entrance to the bay was guarded by nets, with a trawler patrol, but as a matter of fact during the latter part of our stay in Suvla Bay we and the other ships lay at anchor without net protection—a large length had been carried away either by the blizzard or by a transport or supply ship dashing through them. There were no repair nets available, and all that could be done was to put down dummy floats and make believe the nets were there. The scheme thoroughly deceived the German and Austrian submarines, and their praiseworthy lack of initiative was on a par with the rest of their operations in the Eastern Mediterranean. It was officially estimated that no less than forty-five enemy submarines were east of Gibraltar, and the targets

EVACUATION OF SUVLA AND ANZAC 227

offered to them were unparalleled. Apart from the ships of the Navy, there was the enormous traffic plying between Mudros and Salonica to Alexandria and England, and, as was well known to the enemy, most of these freighters, such as store-ships and colliers, were unconvoyed and could not do more than twelve knots. The failure of the enemy submarines was not due to the number of our patrol boats either, as until the end of 1915 these were not plentiful.

The work of the ships in the bay was to support the troops and to keep under the Turkish fire. All our landing places, beaches, and depôts were shelled daily, Sundays especially being marked by heavy firing. There was no spot held by us which was not within range of the enemy guns, and as these were scattered all over the hills in large numbers, only the lack of ammunition saved our troops from being shelled into the sea and our ships out of the harbour.

Each day was much the same, the only difference being in the intensity of the shelling of both sides, but no day passed during which we did not fire many rounds of 6-inch and sometimes 12-inch. Occasionally the Turkish gunners fired at us and then at the transports, but they never scored a hit, though it was a near thing once or twice and splinters of shells were found on board. Great care was taken of everyone, for there had been so many cases in ships of men being killed and wounded when they were merely onlookers, with no deck duties at all. While we were at Suvla the *Glory* had two men killed by a shell and several wounded who thought themselves safe on the lee side of the ship. Directly a shell was seen pitching within any distance of us the long "G" was sounded, and it was fourteen days number ten punishment for anyone found outside armour. One morning we took cover four times.

On one of the days in early December the Commander, Colin Sarel, was lifted off his feet and thrown down by the blast from one of our own 6-inch guns, which was fired as he and Mr. Murphy, the Bo'sun, stood close to the muzzle. It damaged his ears so much that he was sent to Malta and later to England. Mr. Murphy also suffered from severe concussion, and was transferred to Malta. Lieutenant-Commander Stewart, the First-Lieutenant, took over the duty of Commander and shortly afterwards received the acting rank.

An amusing incident of the great storm was reported from West Beach. During the height of the blizzard a small lighter went ashore on a shoal with a crew of seven or eight. It was impossible to go to their rescue for some time, and it was supposed that no stores were on board, no fuel either, and the cold was perishing. At last a rescue party swam out from the shore and found the stranded men in a heap on the deck. Artificial respiration was tried, but to no purpose, and, since there was nothing else to be done, lifebelts were put on them and they were towed to the shore. A doctor and a stomach-pump was requisitioned—the cargo had been rum! This beautiful story was told—by a soldier, of course—in the Ward-room mess.

December 7th was a day of contrasts. Instead of " Evening Quarters," " Action Stations " was sounded off. A bombardment had been arranged for all ships present, including two monitors, on a larger scale than usual. Our own objective was the Pimple Hill, on which we fired, at a range of eight thousand yards, twenty 12-inch and seventy-three 6-inch. It was a magnificent sight to see the bursting lyddite throw up dense clouds of yellow smoke intermingled with dust and earth in a small area, and the accuracy of the shooting could not have been better. The first shot was right on the point of aim, and the official military report said it was the best shooting done by the navy in Suvla. This was pleasing, as on our arrival our firing was more than erratic; the guns shot short, and we dropped at least four rounds in our own lines, luckily without damage. We received a very sarcastic signal from a battery over one shell that did not burst: " We have one of your shells in camp. You can have it on application." For a short while this mishap puzzled the experts, until it was discovered that our guns with well-worn rifling would not take a shell fitted with a certain kind of driving band.

Bishop Price, from China, came on board and confirmed two boys, having journeyed from Mudros on purpose. It is interesting to know that during the Bishop's three months' sojourn at Gallipoli he confirmed six hundred soldiers.

We studied the position on shore and the maps, and tried to make out how things stood with us, and in our humble judgment there was no future except by enormous sacrifices. The Walcheren expedition and its conclusion was analogous— military failure and sickness, followed by the despatch to Spain of our forces and a campaign designated the "Spanish Ulcer" by Napoleon. The similitude was very complete. Well, of course we expected an immediate decision as to the future of the Suvla show. Sometimes one can advance by going back. We read a great deal in the home papers of the disastrous effect a withdrawal would have on the Mohammedan world. Rubbish! The Turks knew—none so well—we were the better men, and that it was merely a question of effort renewed again and again to carry the job. But—was it worth it?

We could read some signs of the times, and after that began guessing.

Turkish prisoners reported that a German officer had arrived at Suvla with four 25-centimetre guns, for which concrete emplacements were being made, and that four still larger were being placed in position at Kum Keoui; but that it was not intended to fire with the first lot until the second was ready, for fear of frightening the ships away. They evidently hoped to do us some damage.

All this time there were rumours that Suvla and Anzac were to be evacuated. We had a pretty shrewd idea, before ever we went to

Suvla, that the great adventure was afoot, and after observation and putting two and two together we were dead sure. On December 9th matters crystallized, and orders were received that the evacuation was to be completed by the 20th of the month. No operation at the Dardanelles gave rise to more speculations as to the probability of success or failure, for, though the original landing and the movements at Salonica had a more world-wide significance, to the tens of thousands involved this withdrawal was the most interesting problem that had ever engrossed their minds. It was unique in history. There was no precedent. And its success staggered the judgment of the most optimistic.

Our Captain, as S.N.O., Suvla, shared in formulating the plans so far as they touched the navy—his special part being the organization and direction of gunfire from all ships in harbour. The *Prince George* was the only other battleship on the spot.

The problem was: How to embark a force of seventy thousand men in sight of an enemy who could bring up troops which would outnumber ours by at least 2 to 1; who held every commanding position; who could shell at will each approach

A PARTING SHOT FROM THE TURKS. SHELL BURSTING CLOSE TO H.M.S. "CORNWALLIS". (*page* 242).

*Central News, Ltd.*

*Central News, Ltd.*

H.M.S. "CORNWALLIS," FIRING AT THE TURKS IN THE MOUNTAINS AFTER THE EVACUATION OF SUVLA (*page* 242).

EVACUATION OF SUVLA AND ANZAC 233

to the beaches and all piers; and who by daily practice had the exact range ?

All retreats are dangerous undertakings, and this re-embarkation of troops from the positions held was one of the most hazardous. So perilous was it that Sir Ian Hamilton refused, according to credible report, to take such a risk, saying that he could not expect to lose less than fifty per cent. of his forces, and his successor in command, Sir Charles Munro, was prepared to lose as a minimum fifteen per cent. These figures show something of the anxiety with which, from the highest to the lowest, the undertaking was approached.

Two elements were essential for success—fine weather and secrecy. The former was there in perfection, and the latter had been preserved in some wonderful way. It was wonderful, for the evacuation had been the common talk of every sailor and soldier for three weeks or more, and an effort to draw the immediate attention of the enemy to such a possibility had been made in the House of Lords. Yet, from subsequent events, it is certain that the Turk and his German adviser had no inkling that any move was in preparation.

Though the actual orders for evacuation were given but eleven days beforehand, elaborate arrangements for the defensive on the retreat had been in progress for some time. Across the promontory of Suvla itself a line of trenches had been dug with maxim gun emplacements, retiring trenches and firing platforms, and this line, when the terrain allowed, was thrice tiered. Hooped wire with strands of barbed intertwined was laid in front of the position, and the same kind of defence was adopted between the Salt Lake and Anzac Bay; so that, as far as Suvla was concerned, this third line protected the whole of the evacuating force. Behind this again local defences were prepared to protect the actual beaches in case of a final rush by the Turk, and so strong were these defences considered that popularly it was thought there was little risk from direct attacks, the main losses being expected from shell fire. All the last days the Engineers were busy mining every available spot, the front trenches, main roads, and paths.

The higher commands had formulated a plan by which the evacuation was to take place each successive night, the last two being the crucial ones, and no difficulties were expected or any reverse considered likely until it came to withdrawing the last bodies of men. Twenty-one thousand were to embark on the 18th to 19th, and twenty thousand five hundred on the 19th to 20th, half from Suvla and the remainder from Anzac.

Orders were given that certain brigades were to retain so many men for the last two nights, the numbers being less than their nominal strength; the result being that the semi-fit and weaklings were drafted off before the last two days, leaving a picked body of thoroughly able men for the final retreat. These last must have been put to no small strain. To realize it one has only to imagine the feelings of those who night after night watched the gradual shrinking of the numbers holding the first line; and saw the well-filled trenches become emptier and the number of yards to be guarded by each man increase. These "remnants" knew that their supports were disappearing, felt they had lost their defenders the 60-pounders, understood that the number of the field guns was getting less daily.

Each night we saw in the dim moonlight store-ships and small transports come in, and disappear before morning full of guns, lorries, ambulances, horses, mules, and the stores of a big army. Every day we looked for some sign which might show that the Turk was conscious of what was going on. One day he was too quiet, another he was registering on the beaches. Daily we looked at the weather reports. Backwards and forwards the wind shifted from north to south and back again; yet the good weather held. But we never knew till the last man had embarked whether the Turk was aware of the evacuation.

So the silent withdrawal continued in secrecy and fine weather. All transport work was suspended during the day and everything looked normal. The same number of fires were lit, the same number of rounds were fired from ships and field guns; there was the same sniping; and to the outward eye nothing was changed.

When the fateful nights came on, there was no element which was not in favour of our success. The moon was practically full, but thin clouds obscured its lighting powers. The sea was calm and unrippled. The damp rising from the land shrouded the Turkish positions in a thin veil of white mist, and the temperature was such that night exposure was no hardship. So the great venture started.

EVACUATION OF SUVLA AND ANZAC 237

At a short distance from the transports and the piers it was scarcely possible to tell that thousands of men were being carried from the beaches to the ships—the motor lighters moved like shadows across the water. What a chance the Turks missed! A score of H.E. shells in the little harbour; a few shrapnel bursting over the heads of the embarking troops; even one or two common exploding in a man-filled lighter, and a different tale would have had to be told.

The first of the last two nights passed without one hitch. Not a unit failed in its appointed place. Before midnight every one of the eleven thousand five hundred from Suvla Bay was safe on board, without a casualty, and by 1 a.m. the bay was empty of all fresh craft; and the danger of discovery was over for the night.

Think of what might have happened had the Turk found out about the night's evacuation. There were only twenty-one thousand men left, spread over a front of eight miles, including all on transport duty, signallers, gunners, beach parties, and medical units. Suppose these had been attacked all day Sunday by a large force; suppose that a concentrated artillery fire had been opened on them—what state would they have been in to retreat on Sunday night ! Suppose every yard of that, in some places, four-mile retreat had been a rearguard fight; and suppose at the end the Turk had concentrated every gun of the scores available on the embarkation beaches; suppose these possibilities, any one of which it was reasonable to expect might happen, had materialized—what proportion of that " remnant " would have got off in safety ?

All this time the covering ships, the *Prince George* and *Cornwallis* (battleships), monitors *Earl of Peterborough* (12-inch guns), M. 29, M. 31, blister-ship *Theseus*, and destroyers, stood with guns manned ready to answer any enemy artillery.

Sunday passed with the usual heavy Sunday shelling by the Turk. Farther south, in the afternoon, off Helles, for an hour and a half, an exceptionally heavy bombardment by ships and field-guns occupied the attention of the enemy. But in the area of the evacuation there was no unusual movement on either side.

At 6 p.m. it became dark. Transports of all sizes, including the *Hannibal* and *Magnificent* with their turrets removed, destroyers and trawlers, gathered from the mists of nowhere without a light showing, and guided by the Navigating

EVACUATION OF SUVLA AND ANZAC 239

Lieutenants of the men-of-war, Lieutenant Clayton of our ship being one of them, took up their appointed stations.

The few remaining transport mules and horses, the last of the guns, and the more valuable remaining stores, were taken on board, and at 1.30 a.m. the historic retreat from the front trenches began. By 3.30 the signal was received, "Evacuation completed." Every living being, man and animal, was taken off, with, at West Beach, the astoundingly slight casualty of one man wounded in the thigh. General Byng, in command of the northern area, was actually the last man to leave the beach at Suvla.

The whole organization from first to last was one complete success. There was no hurry or confusion or noise. The navy and the army did their best. The transports were to hand, the soldiers ready. But without the constant goodness of Providence during these days, no plans of man could have prevented enormous losses. An Old Testament writer would have described the land mist as a pillar of cloud separating the Crescent from the Cross, the moon as the Israelites' Jehovah looking on and ever present, the clouds as the hiding of His face from man, and the placid waters the calm of the Spirit moving over them.

From the point of view of an onlooker in a ship nothing had been visible. It was only in the early hours of the morning that any spectacular display took place. As a matter of precaution, in case bad weather prevented the withdrawal, enormous supplies of food were left ashore. It is also likely that we had not the means or time to embark the stores. Permission was given us to take what we wanted, and we got off for the benefit of the ship's company nearly seven tons of food, bacon, cheese, dried vegetables, jam, syrup, raisins, preserved meat, Oxo, and butter—a drop in the ocean. All the rest, every kind and sort of provender, tons and tons and tons of it, rations valued at £250,000, were to be burnt. So long as the Turk did not get it all was well.

Not every day of the week can one see a bonfire costing a quarter of a million, and when, after the last soldiers had left, the R.E. company remaining set on fire the great prepared heaps all saturated with oil and interspersed with petrol cans the most magnificent blaze we are ever likely to witness flamed from both sides of the bay.

Lying right in the centre of the bay, opposite

EVACUATION OF SUVLA AND ANZAC 241

what had been the central hospital, was a stranded motor hospital lighter, and during the first ten days of our time at Suvla we made repeated unavailing efforts to get her off. She was too firmly fixed. There was nothing for it but to blow her up. Lieutenant Budgen had all arrangements made, and the cable to fire the charges placed on board was then run out into the bay and buoyed—there was nothing left to do but connect the battery. This was successfully taken in hand immediately after the evacuation, and following on a big explosion flames broke out in the lighter fore and aft, and she added to the general holocaust quite a respectable glare.

As dawn broke the Turks began shelling the fires, probably with the idea of preventing any effort to put them out, and as it became really light they commenced to waste ammunition wholesale. We did the silent laugh then, and it really was ludicrous. Shell after shell they pitched round about the landing-places, rank bad shots most of them, and some fell actually into the fires. What had been our main positions were thoroughly searched with high explosive and shrapnel, and as the ships began firing at daylight we had the extraordinary spectacle of ourselves and the enemy firing at the same objects, stranded lighters, burning stores, piers, and the hospital tents and huts, only we did damage and they did not.

It would be interesting to know the exact time at which the Turks discovered that the trenches in front of them were empty. As we fired a few rounds at the Turkish positions somewhere about 7.30 they started in on us as we lay at anchor and splashed several rounds about the bay, some of which were too close to be pleasant. It may have been that at that moment the enemy realized that nothing but two battleships, a few boats, and an odd patrol vessel, remained in the bay.

All this time we were in ignorance of how things were going at Anzac. We had heard several explosions and heavy firing, and it was with feelings of unutterable relief that we received the general signal saying that the evacuation from Anzac was as successful as that of Suvla, the Anzac casualties being two killed and four wounded, making a total of ten for two days in both places !

It was rather thrilling to ponder over the one or more narrow escapes from discovery. The actual withdrawal of the last men from the trenches had been fixed for 1.30. At Anzac

EVACUATION OF SUVLA AND ANZAC 243

at 1.15 a Turkish deserter gave himself up. A few minutes later and he would have discovered that the trenches were empty.

An ingenious scheme was evolved by which dummy guns and maxims were fired some hours after the trenches were abandoned. Candles of varying lengths were lighted, and as they burnt down these let off explosions at intervals of time which sounded exactly like desultory firing.

A Major in the New Zealand Force told us later of the risks run by the last detachments. His post, an advanced salient called the Apex, was normally held by a garrison of six hundred, and at the last, from 11.30 p.m. to the fateful 1.30 a.m., he was left with thirty-one men only and three maxims. His orders were to hold on at all costs, and on no account to start retiring until 1.30; and he was warned that in the event of an attack the little company would not be able to retreat by the only made road, as it would have to be swept by fire. There remained, in such case, as the one means of escape, the climbing of a rugged and difficult hill.

Major Dunbar, R.F.A. (on General Byng's staff), gave an interesting account of what he saw from the *Theseus* during the day of the 20th.

The *Theseus* was off Anzac during the evacuation, and she remained behind to watch the Turks. At first they came out of their trenches a few at a time, and the *Theseus* held her fire. More and more Turks gathered and in denser formation, and still the ship's gunners kept quiet, until a considerable force gathered in a ravine. Then she opened fire with lyddite. The sighting shot went home, and it was followed by a broadside. Very few of that little lot of the enemy escaped.

Destroyers went into deserted Suvla Bay during the afternoon, and received such a warm reception that they beat a hasty retreat, but not before they had seen the German flag flying over Lala Baba— a tactful acknowledgement of their position among the Turks. A dare-devil plan was afoot to cut the flag down at night, but all the ships were recalled before there was time to carry it out.

The evacuation was a lesson in sea power for Germany to brood over. The navy landed the expedition and kept it on shore for eight months by the fire of naval guns, and the navy brought the military force off. The fact that they never advanced beyond the range of our guns is a circumstance for which those who selected the landing-places are answerable. A combined expedition is a great asset, only a nation that has command of the sea can use it, and the principal feature of such omnipotence is the element of surprise. We surrendered that by our naval attack on the Straits and by our own stupidity in selecting the best defended landing-places in Turkish possession as the ones to land at. " The genius of our nation lies in our ability to extricate ourselves from difficulties of our own creation." We can't remember the philosopher who said so, but he spoke the truth.

There was still the force at Helles, and whether or no we were to attempt the withdrawal feat in that direction was eagerly speculated upon.

And now, since the best-intentioned authors cannot be in two places at once, and we wish to give some idea of what happened on shore at Suvla as the Immortal Gamble drew to a close, we have called Mate Terrill of our ship to our aid. He knows more about the happenings than most. His beach party was the last unit to quit the south pier, and he had put in some weeks at Suvla previous to the evacuation.

# CHAPTER XIV

ASHORE AT SUVLA

MATE TERRILL'S ACCOUNT.

SOME men of the Royal Engineers first put the certainty of evacuation into my mind as they commenced work at the beginning of December on machine-gun emplacements almost outside our mess. A little farther off a fatigue party were building long trenches. What was in the wind? Such occupation could not be for purposes of practice—there was ample opportunity for the real thing a couple of miles farther on.

Two days afterwards we embarked a battalion in "K" boats (as the new motor lighters are called), who were "going for a rest." The next night the remnants of a brigade also "leaving for a rest" went off, and as we could not get all their stores aboard by night we carried on in broad daylight. About the 8th December two more battalions landed to take the place of the

ASHORE AT SUVLA

tired ones, and that was all right, but we still had a deficiency of three thousand two hundred frost-bites who had left after the blizzard, and instead of landing more troops we embarked some.

Then I woke up! I could scarce believe my thoughts—I dared not whisper them. An evacuation was already in progress!

For the next three weeks we were working at top pressure getting rid of surplus ammunition, stores, etc., and I am thankful we had the Turk and not the German to deal with—the latter would certainly have tumbled to the state of affairs. If nothing else, he would have noticed the store-ships in the bay getting lower and lower in the water as the stores were put on board, instead of becoming higher as they would have done had they been discharging instead of loading.

A good story filtered through from Anzac. There a " K " boat alongside the pier was embarking mules when suddenly a Taube appeared overhead out of the anywhere. Instantly the naval officer superintending gave orders for the mules to be taken off again, and all the wily aero-Hun saw was the not unusual sight of mules coming on shore.

Things went on at top speed—none of us had

much rest, and I felt a little curious as to whether any arrangement had been made about taking the naval beach party away at the last, or if we were going to swim for it, as up to now I had received no official notice about anything. It was quite clear to anyone on the beach what was taking place, and I thought, by that time, there could not be very many troops and stores remaining. However, a few days before the 19th December two naval officers appeared on the scene, a Commander and Lieutenant, R.N., and after an introduction I was informed that the Commander would take over the reins of government. The responsibility, which, I must admit, was beginning to weigh rather heavily, was lifted from my shoulders and transferred to Commander X.

After a few councils of war the Commander handed out a written copy of his orders and routine for the final days, Saturday and Sunday, and naturally the orders contained instructions in the event of his being "put out." I found I was to work with the Naval Transport Officer on the south pier, which, after being carried away in the storm, had been reconstructed with feverish haste by the Australian Bridging Section.

ASHORE AT SUVLA

The usual routine went on until the historic Saturday when no day work was done, and at 5 p.m. sharp our beach party assembled at the south pier. I heard " General Quarters " sounded by the ships in the bay—apparently all was merry and bright in their direction. But what about us ! If the Turk got the faintest idea of what we were engaged upon all he had to do was to shell the beaches and piers, of which there was not a square yard he could not reach, with shrapnel, and not fifteen per cent. of our men would get off.

At 6.45 p.m. down came the first batch of troops direct from the front-line trenches, and having got them into the appointed motor lighters, they cast off and went to troop carriers, when the lighters returned. So on throughout the night, the troops coming down at arranged times which fitted in with the arrival of the " K " boats. The same routine was carried out simultaneously at A Beach, West, and Anzac.

At about 4.30 a.m. we all got back to our mess, tired, but very light-hearted over our wonderful success in getting the troops away unobserved, and after a little talk about it all we snatched a couple of hours' sleep.

We were up again and working by seven

o'clock. There were many preparations to make for our final night. The camp at Lala Baba was deserted now, and we had to scrape together a few men to light fires at daybreak as usual—this, of course, was done by the military.

I don't remember whether or no the Turks "strafed" us in the morning of Sunday, but in the afternoon they did so with 8-inch shells. I was at the south pier, and they opened fire first on our 60-pounder batteries on Lala Baba and swept the whole ridge, making some very large holes in the ground. One shell actually hit our pier, but before the smoke had cleared away the Australian Bridging Section were on their way with the necessary repairing gear. Strange to say, the Turkish gunners only fired three shells at the pier—or, at least, that is the number which fell within a reasonable distance of it—and kept on hammering away at Lala Baba.

We had an early tea, naturally very subdued, and each of us was occupied with his own thoughts until the N.T.O. ordered "Evacuation Stations," which gave us something else to wrestle with. With a handshake all round—just as it would have been in a cinematograph film — and good wishes, we took up our stations as on the previous night.

On our way we thought the Turk had some suspicions, as he continued to fire small stuff until it was dark, a thing he was not in the habit of doing; but perhaps it was merely our own highly strung nerves which made it seem as though the firing went on later than usual.

Everything was now on a "split-yarn." The "K" boats were at the pier, and the N.T.O. gave the coxswains some final orders. A "K" boat was anchored a short distance off to convey wounded to the hospital ships, of which there were two to each place of evacuation, and more were lying off Mudros in readiness. In addition there were two horse-boats alongside the shore end of the pier to convey the stretcher cases from the shore; picket-boats, etc., for the walking cases; steamboats and cutters at their appointed stations ready to pick up stragglers in the event of a rear-guard action, and a destroyer to take off the Royal Navy beach personnel.

The R.A.M.C. had a temporary base right on the beach, and at about 6 p.m. some three hundred of the R.A.M.C. arrived, carrying on stretchers saws, knives, and other instruments necessary for their part of the game. I thought it was the first lot of wounded coming down, and had an agreeable surprise, but their mere presence reminded one of what might happen in a short time if the Turk kept his eyes open.

At 6.45 the first batch of troops arrived, and we speedily packed them into "K" boats and sent them off to the troop-carriers in the bay. At 7.45 more men turned up and were dealt with, and everything worked splendidly. At midnight we embarked the guns (60-pounders) and their gunners.

The army now had to depend entirely on the guns of the ships and their own machine guns in case of an attack.

When at 12.45 a.m. we embarked fifty per cent. of the R.A.M.C. I was immensely cheered up. About the same time I sent off the only wounded man we had to the hospital "K" boat. I believe he lost his sight, poor fellow.

The excitement was now at white-heat. Instead of reckoning in thousands of troops to be embarked, we could do so in hundreds. I smile now when I remember that such was the tension that no orders were given above a whisper, and the Turk was at least two and a half miles away at the nearest point.

An officer who superintended the evacuation of

ASHORE AT SUVLA 253

the sick and wounded, a R.N.R. Lieutenant, arrived in his boat, and I asked him how things were going at the other beaches. The only casualty he had had was the one we had sent off. Already we could just see, through the lightening darkness, some of the transports leaving, piloted out by the navigating officers of H.M. ships in the bay. Every transport got away in the dark without an accident—surely a marvel of efficiency and organization.

Time went on, and there was but one boat left at the pier. She had on board, so far as I can remember, the last companies of men belonging to the 11th Division, all the Australian Bridging Section, who were the last of the military to leave— if, indeed, you can call them military, as several of them held masters' certificates and served in the R.A.N.B.S.

Suddenly a huge flame shot up to the sky. It was just 3.45, and a few minutes later several more fires flared. We were expecting it, of course, as we knew that all the stores which could not be got away had to be burnt. It was the greatest fire I have ever seen—it lit up the sky for miles round the bay. I thought they might have waited a little longer before starting the bonfire, as our scheduled time for leaving was 4.30 a.m. However, the beautiful scene served to distract our thoughts a little, and in the meantime we employed our beach party in gathering up rope, stores, etc., anything that would be of use to the enemy. He certainly did not get much—even the sand-bags in all dug-outs had several cuts in them.

At 4.30 the Naval Transport Officer ordered me to get the beach party in the lighters. I reported " All aboard " to him, and he was the last man to leave the south pier, I myself being the last but one.

We now waited three-quarters of an hour, in case there were any stragglers. None turned up, and the order was given to cast off.

The only living thing left behind was a mule which had brought down some medical stores to the boat at C Beach, for there was no room for him. He was given blankets, and about a month's fodder—fodder to right of him, fodder to left of him. There were also the tanks which had been used by us for fresh water for the left-behind to drink from if he was athirst. No cudgel thwacked his sides—he had all at his command. He had forgotten his strenuous past, and had not learned to forecast the future. He was quite happy.

As we passed Nebrunessi Point on our way to the troop carrier I saw our mess and dug-out on fire—the work of my opposite number on C Beach. The Turk was a decent fellow, but for all that our enemy, and we could not leave him more than necessary.

I lay down to rest as soon as I could, feeling worn-out, yet thankful that the operation had been such a success, without the awful carnage of the 25th April, and proud, too, of my little share in the great withdrawal.

## CHAPTER XV

### THE HAND IS PLAYED

ON leaving Suvla the *Cornwallis* went direct to Kephalo, having for the first time in her career at the Dardanelles a destroyer escort. We stayed but a day, as a heavy gale sprang up from the north and drove us to Aliki Bay, on the south side of Imbros.

The evacuation, the good and ill of it, was over and done with. Such a storm as this, coming a few hours earlier, would have set at naught the best-laid plans and turned success to failure in the twinkling of an eye. In the sudden clamour of the wind was barbaric triumph, primeval tribute; not otherwise in these self same waters shouted the warriors of old days who made the glory that was Greece. It was grand to hear the rage and roar of it—it stirred the pulses like a trumpet-call.

Even the short steam round to Aliki Bay was not uneventful. As we were entering between

# THE HAND IS PLAYED

the net defences a small store-ship ran across our bows in the dare-devil sort of fashion of a cheeky little dog bouncing across the path of a bad-tempered mastiff. We tried to avoid her, but there was no time. In the words of an excellent diary kept by one of our A.B.'s, " We could not disgise from ourselves that a Krysis was on us." Fortunately we struck the little vessel an oblique blow, and she thought that as she did not sink she must be undamaged, and put out to sea. But a small store-ship cannot bump a battleship with impunity. Almost at once she turned round, and making straight for the shore, beached herself with a fore-hold filled with water.

We met here for the first time the *Hibernia*, and she took over from us the duty of S.N.O. at Kephalo, which we held for twelve hours only. The *Edgar* was told off to salvage our store-ship, for we were returning to Mudros.

Many rumours were aboard as to our plans. We were going home at once; we were destined for Salonica; we were bound for Egypt; we were ordered to the African coast. Well, we should turn the tables on a few of the reports, for we were certainly going somewhere.

On reaching Mudros we heard for certain that

we were leaving the Eastern Mediterranean Squadron and proceeding to Egypt (as Kipling told you lately, the Navy, when it really gets busy, always " proceeds " anywhere and never humdrum " goes ") to join the flag of the Admiral of the East Indies Squadron.

Christmas Day passed quietly, unobtrusively even. Turkeys and plum-puddings were not to be had in Mudros, and the Christmas mail, which would have saved the situation, had not arrived.

We had orders to embark the Commander-in-Chief of the Army, Sir Charles Monro, and his Staff. They joined us on December 28th, and we should have sailed immediately but that a situation arose which made it necessary for the General to confer with the Vice-Admiral, and we waited until January 1st, when the two were able to meet on board the *Cornwallis*. No doubt the conference was in connection with the evacuation from Helles.

Before we left, the Vice-Admiral gave the Captain a memo., dated December 26th, to read to the ship's company. It ran thus:

" As the *Cornwallis* is now leaving the Eastern Mediterranean Squadron, I take the opportunity of thanking you and your ship's company for the excellent spirit and manner

## THE HAND IS PLAYED

in which the many and onerous duties which they have been set have been carried out.

"I wish all success to the *Cornwallis*, and hope she will have many opportunities of adding to the already honourable record which she has earned whilst serving in the E.M.S.

"J. M. DE ROBECK,
"*Vice-Admiral.*"

The approbation of the Admiral was well deserved. The behaviour of our men, their steadiness, cheerfulness, and general good spirit, merits all the praise we can bestow. We have a large proportion of R.F.R., R.N.R. coastguardsmen and pensioners, mostly from ships sunk before December, 1914, and boys for hostilities only. A real mixed lot at the commencement. But they shook down to as efficient a crew as there was in any ship in the East Mediterranean Squadron. We are very proud indeed of our ship's company, and this is just the time to say so.

The ship had been in the neighbourhood of the Dardanelles for fully ten months. On forty days the enemy had fired at her, and she herself had fired five hundred 12-inch shell and six thousand 6-inch. At times life on board had been as exciting as the most grasping could desire, and at others the dulness, lack of exercise, shortage of fresh food, continuous heat and the fly plague, had made things rather trying. We had shared in all operations in which battleships had been engaged, with the exception of the 18th March attack and anything done at Smyrna, and none of us regretted that our lot in this war was to have taken part in the Dardanelles expedition. It was a failure, unfortunately, but we failed in good spirits. "Experience is a name everyone gives to their mistakes." A costly wisdom was ours, but the ultimate standard by which the disastrous expedition will be judged will be derived from nothing else but experience and observation.

Reasons how and why we failed stand outside the scope of our account. We can only say, as is known to all the world, that the enterprise was undertaken without due regard to the difficulties in the way, that the warnings of neutrals were ignored, and the known defensive fighting powers of the Turks minimized. The expedition was a gamble, a gamble undertaken with insufficient forces—and when such forces did arrive they were always just too late. Just as every defeat is a victory, so every failure is a step to success, and the Saga of the Straits will be sung by our people long years after all who gave it orchestration are dead and turned to dust. It

## THE HAND IS PLAYED

will be chanted in notes of triumph; the master-spirit of heroism displayed will uplift it above all thought of disappointment. No greater feat of arms has been writ in our history; no more wonderful story of indomitable courage—

> " More active-valiant, or more valiant-young,
> More daring, or more bold, is now alive,
> To grace this latter age with noble deeds."

## "DIES IRÆ"

"'A made a finer end and went away."—*Henry V.*, Act II., 3.

H.M.S. *Cornwallis* was torpedoed and sunk by enemy submarine in the Mediterranean on January 9, 1917. Details of the loss it is not permissible to give, but this much we may say, the ship did her best for us like the fine old craft she was, floating long enough to allow the whole ship's company, barring the fifteen men killed in the explosion, to save their lives. The long habit of floating had indisposed the *Cornwallis* from sinking, and for a short time it seemed that we might get her to port. Fate, and the gentle German, was against us.

The behaviour of the officers and men during the last phase was in accordance with the best traditions of the Service, and as for the ship, she was, as she had ever been, a worthy holder of her great name.

To have one's home turn upside down is a bit of an upheaval in the best regulated household, and to see the actual process, since " the house of everyone is to him as his castle and fortress, as well for his defence against injury and violence, as for his repose," is to suffer a shock which all those who understand the true nature of home will appreciate. Two of our officers had spent over five years each in the *Cornwallis*—and five years is a large slice of one's Service life.

The Bos'un's mate piped the old ship down. Just as she was about to take her last voyage, and as all that was left of her slipped reluctantly from our sight, the reed-like notes of the sweetest *Nunc dimittis* a seaman knows floated on the wind.

Thence, on passage perilous, to Malta, and thence—HOME.

# APPENDIX

## LIST OF HONOURS, H.M.S. "CORNWALLIS," DURING 1915.

### V.C.
Midshipman W. St. A. Malleson, R.N.

### D.S.O.
Captain A. P. Davidson, R.N.
Lieutenant J. A. V. Morse, R.N.

### D.S.C.
Lieutenant E. Madge, R.N.R.
Mr. J. Murphy, C.G.M. (R.N.) (Boatswain).
Midshipman M.C.H. Lloyd, R.N.
Midshipman H. M. S. Forbes, R.N.
Midshipman W. H. Monier-Williams, R.N.

### C.G.M.
A. J. Ade, Stoker (specially promoted to Leading Stoker).

### D.S.M.
A. Roake, A.B.
A. Playford, P.O.
A. J. Chatwin, Yeo. Sigs.
E. T. F. Jezzard, Sh. Std.
S. H. Evans, Ord. Teleg.

# APPENDIX 265

CERTIFICATE FOR ZEAL AND DEVOTION TO DUTY, AWARDED BY G.O.C., R.N.D.

D. Lynch, St., R.N.D.

MENTIONED IN DESPATCHES.

Major W. W. Frankis, R.M.L.I.
Lieutenant H. F. Minchin, R.N.
Temporary Surgeon W. D. Galloway, R.N.

ROYAL HUMANE SOCIETY CERTIFICATE FOR LIFE-SAVING.

Temporary Surgeon W. D. Galloway, R.N.
H. Jarvis, P.O.

KILLED, APRIL 25TH, 1915.

| Name. | Rank or Rating. |
|---|---|
| Hardiman, A. M. | Midshipman. |
| Medhurst, W. E. | P.O. |
| Coslett, L. G. | A.B. |
| Dauncey, H. E. | A.B. |
| Grose, E. | A.B. |
| Hughes, W. | A.B. (R.F.R.). |
| Snowden, W. T. | A.B. (R.F.R.). |
| Clements, H. G. | O.S. |
| Curtis, J. E. | O.S. |
| Howe, G. | A.B. |
| Pearson, A. E. | O.S. |
| Rix, G. H. | O.S. |
| Sutherland, D. S. | O.S. |
| Burnett, E. H. | Boy. |
| Hillam, G. H. | Boy. |
| Taylor, W. | A.B. |

## THE IMMORTAL GAMBLE

### DIED OF WOUNDS.

| Name. | Rank or Rating. |
|---|---|
| Coles, F. | A.B. (August 22nd, 1915). |
| Calder, G. T. B. | Ldg. Stoker (August 11th, 1915). |

### DIED OF DISEASE.

| Name. | Rank or Rating. |
|---|---|
| Burden, E. D. | E.R.A. (R.N.R.). |
| Hollows, Fred | Pte. (R.M.L.I.). |

### ACCIDENTALLY KILLED.

| Name. | Rank or Rating. |
|---|---|
| Theodore Joughlin | P.O. |
| Atkins, G. H. A. | Ship's Corporal. |

### WOUNDED ON 25TH APRIL, 1915.

| Name. | Rank or Rating. |
|---|---|
| Lloyd, M. C. H. | Midshipman. |
| Monier-Williams, M. W. H. | Midshipman. |
| Bates, J. | A.B. |
| Bristow, A. | P.O. |
| Burrows, E. | A.B. (R.F.R.). |
| Butler, J. F. | A.B. (R.N.R.). |
| Butterworth, H. S. | A.B. (R.F.R.). |
| Carter, W. A. | A.B. (R.N.R.). |
| Chaulk, E. | A.B. (R.N.R.). |
| Coleman, C. A. | A.B. |
| Cronin, E. P. | Boy. |
| Cutting, C. H. | O.S. |
| Darling, J. T. | Boy. |
| Day, W. | A.B. |

## APPENDIX

| Name. | Rank or Rating. |
|---|---|
| Dorling, D. S. | O.S. |
| Derbyshire, G. | A.B. (R.F.R.). |
| Edwards, W. W. | O.S. |
| Ford, T. C. | L.S. |
| Fry, A. G. | O.S. |
| Flay, W. J. | A.B. (R.N.R.). |
| Goddard, J. J. | O.S. |
| Green, F. | A.B. (R.N.R.). |
| Hallam, G. | Boy. |
| Heal, W. N. | A.B. |
| Holmes, G. | A.B. (R.F.R.). |
| Hull, E. W. | P.O. |
| Lawrence, J. G. | A.B. |
| Leach, J. A. | A.B. (R.F.R.). |
| Lyne, W. G. | A.B. |
| Mackerel, F. W. | O.S. |
| Marsh, T. A. | O.S. |
| McBride, O. | Boy. |
| McIver, A. | A.B. (R.N.R.). |
| Rickus, E. F. | A.B. |
| Roake, H. | A.B. (R.F.R.). |
| Samson, J. A. | A.B. (R.N.R.). |
| Sawyer, F. E. | O.S. |
| Smith, H. G. | A.B. (R.F.R.). |
| Stanley, H. | O.S. |
| Steeley, A. | Boy. |
| Trollope, F. E. | Pte. (R.M.L.I.). |
| Trotter, W. | O.S. |
| Turner, C. G. | Boy. |
| Warren, S. | L.S. (R.N.R., Newfoundland). |

## OFFICERS WHO SERVED IN H.M.S. "CORNWALLIS" BETWEEN DECEMBER, 1914, AND MARCH, 1916.

| Rank. | Name. | Appointed. | Left. |
|---|---|---|---|
| Captain | C. E. Le Mesurier | September 14, 1914 | January 21, 1915 |
| ,, | A. P. Davidson, D.S.O. | January 21, 1915 | * |
| Commander | C. A. M. Sarel | October 16, 1914 | December 19, 1915 |
| ,, (Act.) | A. T. Stewart | September 9, 1914 | * |
| Lieutenant-Commander (Emerg.) | A. V. Courage | November 1, 1914 | * |
| Lieutenant (N.) | J. W. Clayton | September 9, 1914 | * |
| ,, (G.) | H. F. Minchin | September 24, 1914 | * |
| ,, (T.) | D. A. Budgen | September 9, 1914 | * |
| ,, | J. A. V. Morse, D.S.O. | November 14, 1914 | July 29, 1915 |
| ,, | J. W. Riddle | September 21, 1914 | February, 1915 |
| ,, | E. S. Williams | July 30, 1915 | August 29, 1915 |
| ,, (E.) | C. Milward | June 15, 1915 | August, 1915 |
| ,, (E.) | S. J. Herbert | August 31, 1915 | December 25, 1915 |
| Lieutenant-Commander (R.N.R.) | B. G. Drake (ret.) | November, 1914 | January 18, 1915 |
| ,, | J. W. C. Venn | November, 1914 | July 27, 1915 |
| ,, | E. E. Madge, D.S.C. | January 24, 1915 | January 19, 1916 |
| ,, Lieutenant (R.N.R.) | W. L. Rosseter | September 6, 1915 | * |
| ,, | F. Pickering | December 24, 1915 | * |
| ,, | V. C. Bowles | October 25, 1915 | * |
| ,, | D. H. Bryant | February 27, 1916 | * |
| ,, | M. M. Frankis | November, 1914 | June, 1915 |
| Major (R.M.) | A. M. M. Shewell | July 9, 1915 | * |
| Captain (R.M.) | E. M. C. Parker | November, 1914 | * |
| Lieutenant (R.M.) | W. H. Crichton | June 30, 1911 | * |
| Engineer-Commander | S. W. Cooke | October 7, 1914 | July 8, 1915 |
| Engineer-Lieutenant-Commander (Emerg.) | F. L. Newhouse | September 23, 1914 | * |
| Chaplain | Rev. C. J. E. Peshall, B.A. | December 1, 1914 | * |
| ,, | J. H. Lightfoot | October 21, 1914 | * |
| Fleet-Surgeon | | November 1914 | |

# APPENDIX

| | | | |
|---|---|---|---|
| Surgeon (R.N.V.R.) | L. C. P. Irvine | October 21, 1914 | December 21, 1915 |
| Sub-Lieutenant | E. O. T. Keeling | November 20, 1914 | * |
| Mate | F. Terrill | December 24, 1915 | * |
| Assistant Paymaster (R.N.R.), Temp. | T. Dell | November, 1914 | * |
| ,, ,, | T. H. Holland | November 6, 1915 | July 1, 1915 |
| ,, ,, | L. C. Patterson | January 12, 1915 | * |
| Chief Carpenter | J. Uglow | September, 1914 | November 25, 1915 |
| Chief Gunner | P. Crennell | October, 1914 | * |
| ,, ,, | C. G. McCarthy | January 5, 1916 | * |
| Gunner (Act.) | T. J. Worrell | December 13, 1914 | * |
| Gunner-Torpedo (Act.) | J. C. Swayne | January 9, 1916 | * |
| Boatswain | J. Murphy, D.S.C., D.C.M. | September 20, 1914 | * |
| Boatswain (Act.) | R. G. Young | December 11, 1914 | April 1, 1915 |
| Boatswain (Act.) | M. Spillane | December 11, 1914 | August 27, 1915 |
| Boatswain (Act.) | S. H. Luxon | | |
| | (Promoted from C.P.O.) | | |
| Artificer-Engineer | W. C. Abbie | July, 1914 | * |
| ,, ,, | A. W. Purcell | September 24, 1914 | * |
| Artificer-Engineer (Act.) | T. G. Stevens | | March 16, 1916 |
| | (Promoted from C.E.R.A.) | | |
| Warrant-Engineer (R.N.R.) | J. W. Lawson | November 27, 1914 | * |
| Midshipman | A. M. Hardiman (killed) | December, 1914 | April, 1915 |
| ,, | M. G. Edwards | December, 1914 | * |
| ,, | H. M. S. Forbes, D.S.C. | December, 1914 | * |
| ,, | D. W. H. Last | December, 1914 | * |
| ,, | M. C. H. Lloyd, D.S.C. | December, 1914 | * |
| ,, | V. J. Voelcker | December, 1914 | * |
| ,, | H. E. E. Weblin | December, 1914 | * |
| ,, | P. A. W. Waite | December, 1914 | * |
| ,, | W. St. A. Malleson, V.C. | December, 1914 | April 25, 1915 |
| ,, | W. H. Monier-Williams, D.S.C. | December, 1914 | * |
| Clerk | K. W. James | November 7, 1914 | |

* Still serving in March, 1916.

PRINTED IN GREAT BRITAIN BY
BILLING AND SONS, LTD., GUILDFORD

www.ingramcontent.com/pod-product-compliance
Lightning Source LLC
Chambersburg PA
CBHW060456090426
42735CB00011B/2005